ISBN 978-1-334-26207-4
PIBN 10760206

1 MONTH OF
FREE
READING

at
www.ForgottenBooks.com

By purchasing this book you are eligible for one month membership to ForgottenBooks.com, giving you unlimited access to our entire collection of over 700,000 titles via our web site and mobile apps.

To claim your free month visit:
www.forgottenbooks.com/free760206

r Liberty in Christ

A Study in Galatians

By

Philip Mauro

HAMILTON BROS.

SCRIPTURE TRUTH DEPOT

120 Tremont Street

Boston, Mass.

Contents

I.

"THE GRACE OF CHRIST"
(Gal. 1 :6)

The substance of the message of Paul to the churches of Galatia is found in the words "Our liberty which we have in Christ" (2:4). We purpose, therefore, to inquire into the meaning of that expression. As one meditates upon it, such questions as the following arise in the mind: What is the nature of the "liberty" referred to? How is it secured, and how enjoyed? What are the dangers that threaten it? and how may one who has received it be brought again "into bondage"? or be "entangled again with the yoke of bondage"? It will surely be found both interesting and profitable to seek light from the Word of God upon these matters; and in this quest the reader of these pages is invited to join.

There is special need for such an inquiry as this, because of the uncertainty among God's people as to the precise nature of their liberty in Christ, and as to what they have been freed from.

That the Epistle to the Galatians has to do chiefly with our liberty in Christ, and that its purpose is to safeguard that precious liberty by raising a warning against the dangers which threaten to rob us of it, is easily seen. The contrast between "liberty" and "bondage" runs all through the Epistle. Moreover, the conclusion which the apostle draws from the remarkable "allegory" in chap. 4

is that "we are not children of the bondwomen but of the *free*"; he having shown by the comparison between Abraham's two families, that whereas the earthly Jerusalem "is *in bondage* with her children," the "Jerusalem which is above is *free,* which is the mother of us all" (4:25, 26, 31). Furthermore, this allegory gives occasion for the stirring exhortation addressed to the people of God: "Stand fast therefore in *the liberty* wherewith Christ hath *made us free,* and be not entangled again with the yoke of bondage" (5:1). And again a little further on it is said: "For, brethren, ye have been called *unto liberty*" (5:13).

The same idea of the liberty wherewith Christ has made us free is expressed in other forms of words. Thus, a parallel to the phrase "called unto liberty" is found in chap. 1 verse 6,, in the expression "called * * into the grace of Christ." These parallel expressions afford much help in our efforts to arrive at the meaning of the Spirit's message in this portion of Scripture. Believers are "called into" (or unto) something which is described as "our liberty in Christ," and also as "the grace of Christ," as "the truth of the gospel," and again as "the faith of the Son of God," and by yet other phrases. That which *calls* them into this new state of existence (a state as different from the old as liberty is different from bondage) is "the gospel." The one who thus "called" the Galatians was Paul the apostle, as appears by the words: "I marvel that ye are so soon removed from him that *called you* into the grace of Christ" (1:6); and by the words: "This persuasion cometh not of *him that calleth you*" (5:8).

It further appears that the word "liberty," as used in

this portion of Scripture, defines the conditions of life and the privileges that pertain to *children* in a household, as contrasted with the condition of *bond-servants*. By taking notice of these leading points we shall find it comparatively easy to understand the scope of the Epistle as a whole, and to understand also certain passages which otherwise would be obscure or even meaningless.

But there is a matter to which we ought to give earnest heed, and which is of greater importance even than the *meaning* of the Scriptures we propose to study; and that is the *lesson* those Scriptures are intended to convey. By the *lesson* we mean that which is given for the purpose of shaping our conduct, of directing us in the *doing* of the will of God, and conforming us in our behaviour to the image of His Son. God's communications to men have ever a *practical* object; and this important fact we deem it necessary to emphasize as strongly as possible, since it is often overlooked. It is natural for men to seek knowledge or information for its own sake, for the pleasure which the quest of knowledge gives, and for the satisfaction which the possession of it imparts. For "knowledge puffeth up" (1 Cor. 8:1); and this is true of Bible knowledge as of other sorts.

On the other hand, it is *quite contrary* to the nature of man to seek information from God *for the purpose of doing God's will in place of his own.* Hence man will listen with interest and even pleasure to addresses in which Scriptures are expounded, dispensations are explained, prophecies interpreted, and the like; but "they will not endure sound *doctrine*" (2 Tim. 4:3). A writer commenting on Stephen's address and the quiet attention given by his hearers to the first part of it, says: "Up to this point the argument was interesting. *People will always admire an academic sermon which leaves themselves untouched.*" And this trait of human nature is well understood by preachers who have an eye to the advantages of popularity. There are those who, by judicious selection of themes, and care in the manner of preaching them, can even be to a certain extent *scriptural* and at the same time "please men." But Paul was not a preacher of that sort, and here we have the striking proof of it in that the Galatians, whom he had called into the grace of Christ, were being removed or drawn away from him, and for the reason that he sought not to please men; "for," he said, "if I yet pleased men, I should not be the servant of Christ" (1: 10).

We are deeply convinced that the people of God are suffering woefully at this present moment for lack of *teaching;* and not only for lack of real "teaching" *in the Bible sense of that word,* but because also they are being plentifully supplied from pulpit and platform, and by means of books and magazines, with something *called* "teaching," which in fact is *not teaching at all.* There are at this time in their hands many readable and interesting expositions of Galatians, Ephesians, and other portions of the Word of God, which practically *ignore the lessons thereof.* Such expositions are worse than useless; for they make the people of God *think* they are being *taught,* when in fact the teaching, which is the *vital thing,* is slighted, if not altogether omitted.

We believe that what is chiefly lacking in the ministry the people of God are receiving at the present time is *teaching,* and that the evils which are manifest among us are due largely to that lack.

We read of Ezra that he had "prepared his heart to seek the *law* of the Lord and to *do* it, and to *teach* in Israel *statutes* and *judgments*" (Ezra 7:10). So likewise the Lord Jesus Christ, when He opened His mouth and "*taught*" His disciples, gave them—not expositions of the Scriptures or interesting addresses thereon, but—the *commandments* which they were to *keep* (Mat. 5:2). And it is recorded that when He had finished His sayings, "the people were astonished at His *doctrine* (*i. e.,* teaching); for He *taught* them as One having *authority*" (Mat. 7:28, 29).

Briefly then, "teaching" consists in telling the people of God what they ought to *do;* and the qualified "teacher" is one who *himself* does the things which he teaches. Ezra sought the law of the Lord first to do it himself, and then to teach others. Christ promises rewards to those who "*do* and teach" His commandments (Mat. 5:19). He Himself is the great Example in all things. He spent thirty years *doing* the things that were well-pleasing in the sight of God, before He began to *teach.* Hence Luke refers to "all that Jesus began to *do* and teach" (Acts 1:1).

Paul was such a teacher. He wrote to the Corinthians concerning Timothy, saying: He shall bring you into remembrance of *my ways which be in Christ,* as I *teach everywhere in every church*" (1 Cor. 4:17). Timothy was equipped for this task, for Paul could write to him "Thou hast fully known my *doctrine, manner of life,* faith," etc. (2 Tim. 3:10). To the Philippians he said:

"Those things which ye have both learned and received and heard, and *seen in me,* do." (Phil. 4:9).

The *teaching,* then, or in other words, "the *doctrine* of Christ" which Paul pressed so earnestly upon the Galatians, had to do not with orthodox views concerning the ground on which sinners are forgiven, but *with the manner in which the children of God ought to live.* Such indeed is the "doctrine" of all the Scriptures; for while that which is variously called "the doctrine of Christ" or "the apostles' doctrine," or "the doctrine of God our Saviour," or the "sound doctrine," is one complete body of truth, it comprehends many details, some being found in one part of the Word and some in another. But whatsoever they be, and wheresoever they are found, their purpose always is *the perfecting of the saints in* the *doing* of the will of God our Father. For God purposes to have a family of children having the family likeness of His own Son, as He Himself said: "For whosoever shall *do the will of My Father which is in heaven,* the same is My brother, and sister, and mother" (Mat. 12:50. Comp. John 6:38; and Heb. 10:9).

The Lord Jesus puts before our eyes the strongest possible inducement for the doing of His commandments, saying, "Ye are *My friends* if ye *do whatsoever I command you.*"

In the case of the Galatians it is recorded that they were "all the sons of God by faith in Jesus Christ"; but the trouble was that they were being misled as, to their "walk," or behaviour. They had come under the influence of teachers who were leading them into the *doing* of certain things which were contrary to "the truth of the gospel." It was not at all a question of orthodoxy, that is to say, correct opinions, or right views *about* the truth, but altogether a matter of *"obeying* the truth." Right views of truth are indeed essential, for without them there would be no rules for right conduct. But correct views and information as to Divine things are of no avail at all, except so far *as they are wrought out in the life.*

What we have thus indicated as to the lesson of Gala tians will become quite clear as we examine the text of the Epistle, which we now proceed to do.

It is noticeable that Paul lays great stress at the outset upon the fact that his apostleship, or in other words his commission and authority as a messenger to the nations of the world, was bestowed upon him, not by or through the agency of man, but directly by Jesus Christ and God the Father Who raised Him from the dead. There was no pride in this assertion of and insistence upon the Divine Source of his apostleship; for nothing was farther from his thoughts than to demand or to accept any honor from men, or to exalt himself in any way. Paul's own estimate of himself as an apostle is expressed in what he wrote to the church at Corinth: "For I am the least of the apostles, that am not meet to be called an apostle, because I persecuted the church of God" (1 Cor. 15:9).

It was highly important, however, for *those to whom Paul delivered his message,* that they should know with certainty that it (the message or "gospel" which Paul terms "my gospel") was altogether Divine in its origin, in its authority, and in its substance. Hence he is at much pains in chapter 1 to make it plain first *negatively* that the gospel he preached was "not after man," since he had **not**

received it of man or been taught it by man; and then
affirmatively, that he *had* received it "by the revelation of
Jesus Christ." This, indeed, was part of the Lord's purpose in appearing in Person to this "chosen vessel," who
was to bear His Name "before the Gentiles, and kings,
and the people of Israel" (Acts 9:15). It was His wise
plan that Gentiles, equally with Jews, should hear the
truth of the resurrection from one who was an eye-
witness and an ear-witness of Christ. The words spoken
to Paul by Ananias in Damascus make this very plain.
Ananias said: "The God of our fathers hath chosen thee,
that thou shouldst know His will, and *see* that Just One,
and shouldst *hear* the voice of His mouth. For thou shalt
be His witness unto all men of what thou has *seen* and
heard" (Acts 22:14, 15).

It is sometimes supposed that because Paul used the expression "my gospel" (Rom. 2:16; 16:25; 2 Tim. 2:8),
he preached a different gospel to that preached by the
other apostles of Christ; but there is quite enough evidence in the Epistle to the Galatians, without reference to
many other Scriptures, to prove that there is but *one*
gospel—"the gospel of God concerning His Son"—for all
the world. For the preaching of "another gospel" is
here denounced in the strongest terms. In chapter 2:14,
Paul, speaking of Peter and others, says: "But when I
saw that they walked not uprightly according to the truth
of the gospel," etc. This shows that there was but one
and the same gospel for all. The expression "my gospel" as used by Paul means simply that message to
which he had been "separated" or specially set apart by
God (Rom. 1:1-4). Any other of the apostles, and any

other man whom God may call to the preaching of the gospel, could with equal right use the same expression.

What the apostle says of the Lord Jesus Christ in his introductory words gives a clear indication of the subject with which he was specially burdened. These are the words: "Who gave Himself for our sins that He might *deliver us* from *this present evil world* (or age) according to the will of God and our Father." It is not Christ's delivering us from judgment and the wrath to come (1 Th. 1:10) nor yet His bringing us to God (1 Pet. 3:18), that the apostle here mentions in speaking of the Lord's death for His people; but that He might deliver us *now,* during the time of our existence in the mortal body, from this present evil world. The special purpose of Christ's death on our behalf that is here pressed upon our attention is that we might be brought into a state of being free from all the influence of this evil age, wherein our "walk" or manner of life should be not only different from that which is shaped by the customs and conventions of the world (particularly the religious world), but in fact *directly contrary thereto.* And this is "according to the will of God and our Father" The words "our Father" are significant, since they point to the fact that the Epistle is, in a special way, a communication to the Lord's people in their relation to God as His *children.*

The "bondage" therefore from which Christ died to set us free, is *bondage to the world and its ways.* Even the law of God could not deliver from that bondage, for Paul says that they (the Israelites) before Christ came, "were *in bondage* under the elements of the world" (4:3).

That the apostle was writing under a strong pressure,

and was deeply stirred because of the grave danger to which the churches of Galatia were exposed, is apparent from the abrupt manner in which he plunges into his subject. "I marvel," he says, "that ye are so soon removed from him that called you into the grace of Christ, unto another gospel, which is not another."*

Close attention should be paid to these words, for their purport is sometimes misunderstood. What is chiefly to be noted is that the term "gospel," as here used, has a much broader signification than is ordinarily given to it in modern usage. By the word "gospel" is now usually meant God's message to the unsaved, which declares the forgiveness of sins through the redemption that is in Christ Jesus, and calls upon all men everywhere to repent. But "the gospel" includes much more than God's message and call to the unconverted; and in the Scripture before us it plainly refers in particular to the doctrine or truth of God *whereby His saints are to live.* "The gospel of God," in the broad sense of that word, embraces *God's complete message* for this age, both to the saved and the unsaved. The error into which the Galatians were being led was not in regard to the message which sinners are to believe in order to receive forgiveness of sins—that Christ died for our sins, and was buried, and rose again the third day—but was an error concerning that part of the gospel *which is to be obeyed by the saints of God,* and which is to shape their entire manner of life. The teaching to which they were giving heed was designed to lead them

---

*The apparent contradiction "another gospel which is not another" does not exist in the original, where two different words (both translated "another") are used. The sense is "a *different* gospel which is *not another*"—for there is but one gospel for all the world of sinners, whether Jews or Gentiles.

—not into a denial of the fact of Christ's sacrifice for sin, or of its sufficiency as a ground of forgiveness, or of His bodily resurrection from the dead, but—into the *doing* of things that were contrary to "the truth of the gospel." Therefore we should take careful note of the things against which the Spirit of God raises here so strong a protest.

In chapter 2 Paul refers to the fact that, while he was in Jerusalem, he had refused to yield to those who insisted that believers from among the Gentiles be circumcised, and his declared object in withstanding that doctrine was "that *the truth of the gospel* might *continue* with you" (2:5). It was not that circumcision mattered either one way or the other, for "circumcision is nothing and uncircumcision is nothing"; but that a vital principle was involved, since *"the keeping of the commandments of God"* is everything (1 Cor. 7:19). We should therefore spare no effort to lay hold of the principle for which the apostle was at that time so zealously contending; for the principle is of as much importance now as it was then.

Further light on this point (namely, that we have to do here with the gospel for *saints,* not with the gospel for *sinners*) may be had from verse 14 of chapter 2, already referred to, where Peter's conduct, which Paul was constrained in faithfulness to the Lord to rebuke "before them all," is spoken of as not walking "uprightly according to *the truth of the gospel."* Here again it is clearly seen that "the truth of the gospel" which was at stake, concerns not the good news by which sinners are brought to Christ, but the *commandments* in which the saints are to walk uprightly all their days on earth.

Such being the point of God's message through Paul to the churches of Galatia, it should be easy for all who have spiritual discernment to perceive the great need for the preaching of the same message to His people who are now in the world. For there be many who, though they are quite clear as to God's way of salvation for sinners, display nevertheless a very imperfect comprehension of the way in which His saints should walk, according to "the doctrine of Christ," recorded in the Gospels as coming from His own lips, and unfolded, amplified and applied in specific details, in the Epistles inspired by the Holy Spirit.

For centuries of time (during the middle ages) the christianized nations lay in utter darkness as to God's way of salvation for perishing sinners. But at the Reformation the knowledge of that way was recovered; and during the subsequent centuries it has been set forth with ever increasing clearness. For this we cannot be too thankful. But at the same time it behoves us to take notice of another tendency that has accompanied the recovery of light as to God's way of salvation. Prior to the Reformation the universally accepted doctrine of Christendom was that of the Church of Rome, namely, that salvation was to be had solely through the sacraments and ceremonies of "the church," and through the religious "works" (penances and the like) of the sinner himself. In other words, the knowledge of salvation from sin and judgment *by grace alone,* to be received through simple faith, had been virtually blotted out. Inasmuch as the religious works which the false "church" laid upon the sinner for the attainment of his own salvation were called

"good works," it is not to be wondered at that the recovery of the doctrine of pure *grace* had the effect of producing, in many, an aversion even to the very mention of
"good works."   This reaction against "good works" on
the part of those who came to understand that salvation
is by God's grace alone, apart from works of law, was
foreseen; and hence the very Scripture which says: "For
by grace are ye saved *through faith,* and that not of yourselves, it is the gift of God," goes on immediately to
declare that those who are saved by God's grace "are
created (anew) in Christ Jesus *unto good works* which
God hath before ordained (*i. e.* prepared) that we should
walk in them" (Eph. 2:8-10).

We establish therefore the fact that "the grace of
Christ" into which the gospel brings us, is *a state of being,*
or a *manner of life,* which (according to God's plan) is
to be characterized by "good works."   Those works, however, are not works *of law,* but works *of faith*—things
done in obedience to "the law of Christ" (6:2).   They
are to be done, moreover, not in order to secure the forgiveness of sins and the bestowal of eternal life, but for
the very different reason that pardon and life *have been
already secured to us* by the death of our Lord Jesus
Christ as a sacrifice for us.   Therefore we keep His com
mandments *because we love Him,* remembering His
words: "He that hath *My commandments and keepeth
them,* he it is that loveth Me," and "He that loveth Me
not keepeth not My sayings" (John 14: 21, 24).

II

"ANOTHER GOSPEL"

The Galatians were being removed (or literally *changed*) from the grace of Christ unto a different gospel which is not another. Apparently they had not actually abandoned the ground to which the apostle's preaching and teaching had brought them, and which he called (in writing to the Corinthians) "the gospel * * wherein ye *stand*" (1 Cor. 15:1) ; but they were *being* seduced therefrom by teaching which Paul here refers to as "a different gospel" (since it opposes the gospel of God) and as "not another" (since in reality it was not "gospel" at all, but a legal system of vain religious works, a system which moreover the true gospel had, by God's decree, wholly abolished and displaced).

God's purpose for those whom He called in His grace is not accomplished at their conversion. *It is then only begun.* Conversion (bringing pardon and eternal life) is not *the end* of God's dealings with a sinner: it is only *the beginning.* Life is given in order that *the purposes of life* may be fulfilled, and the works thereof accomplished; for God creates everything with a definite object. The Galatians had *begun well;* for they had "begun in the Spirit" (3:1, 3). The gospel of Christ had been preached unto them in the power of the Spirit; they had been convicted of sin, had repented, had believed in Jesus Christ, had been born again, and had been baptized (3:26, 27). They were "Christ's," and hence were "Abraham's

seed and heirs according to *the* promise" (3 : 29). Moreover, Paul witnesses that they "did run well" at the first
(5 : 7). But they had been "troubled" and hindered in
their progress by some who would "pervert the gospel
of Christ." This is what we wish to look into.

The danger was not only very real, but very great. Paul
was deeply moved with concern on their behalf lest he
should have bestowed upon them "labour in vain"
(4 : 11). He saw the possibility of all the results of his
toil being swept away by the menacing flood of unsound
doctrine. This, of course, refers not to his labour in
bringing them to Christ, but to that expended in teaching
and training them in the right ways of the Lord;
for, being the children of God, they could not be *lost*.
Moreover, their spiritual condition, resulting from the activities of these false teachers, was such that Paul says he
travailed, as it were, in birth for them again, not (be it
noted) to the end that they might be converted or born
again from above, but that Christ might be *formed in
them* (4 : 19).

Only a very serious danger, involving consequences
disastrous in character, could have caused such solicitude
for those beloved saints, whom Paul affectionately calls
"my little children"; or could have given rise to such
mighty spiritual strivings on their behalf (Comp. Col.
1 : 29).

But the most eloquent and convincing testimony to the
seriousness of the conditions then developing among the
churches of Galatia is found in the remarkable *denuncia-
tions* pronounced against anyone—be he an apostle on
earth or an angel from heaven—who should preach any

other gospel than that which Paul himself had preached. Twice we read the awe-inspiring sentence of judgment, "Let him be accursed."

Those solemn words tell clearly what is God's estimate of the value of His gospel, and in what light He regards the activities of any, however exalted their rank, who seek, even though it be in mistaken religious zeal, to substitute for it a different gospel. And we need to keep always in mind the fact that what is here so vehemently denounced as the preaching of "another gospel," is not God's message to sinners but to *saints*—the children of God. This should deeply impress all who are charged with responsibility for ministry of the Word to the people of God; for it witnesses powerfully to the vital importance, in God's eyes, of the *sound doctrine* which He has provided in the words and commandments spoken by the Lord Jesus Christ, and has explained and applied through the Epistles of Paul and other apostles. This appalling denunciation adds impressively to the significance of the charge which Paul gave to Timothy, touching the same matter, namely, the doctrine given to the people of God. As for example in the following passages:

"If thou put the brethren in remembrance of these things"—*i. e.,* things to be *done,* not mere matters of opinion—"thou shalt be a good minister of Jesus Christ, nourished up in the words of faith and of *good doctrine*" (1 Tim. 4:6).

"If any man *teach* otherwise"—referring to *commandments* to believers who were bond-servants— "and consent not to wholesome words, even *the words of our Lord Jesus Christ* and to the *doctrine that is according to godliness,* he is proud, knowing nothing, but doting about questions and strifes of words," etc. (id., 6:3, 4).

There can be no doubt then that what was at stake was a thing of immense value in God's eyes; and it is clear also that it was a thing affecting, not the conversion of sinners, but the perfecting of saints.

If we inquire why the matter which prompted the writing of this Epistle was of such importance and urgency, we shall find two reasons appearing prominently in the text. In the first place, *the work of God in the Galatian saints was being hindered.* They were being turned out of the way that leads to growth, maturity and fruitfulness, into a vain and empty life of "bondage." But of even far greater moment is the fact that, in departing from "the grace of Christ" to which they had been called, they were virtually *setting at naught what Christ had accomplished for them by His death on the cross.* This should be carefully considered, for it explains the intensity of the apostle's language, both in tone and substance; and, above all, it bears witness to the supreme value of the Cross of Christ, and of all that He suffered to accomplish by it.

Let us then note that the Galatians were being led into certain religious doings having for their professed object the accomplishment of results which had been *already secured to believers through the cross*—results which could be accomplished in no other way. Those believers had been given access by faith, through the work of the Lord Jesus Christ, into that grace wherein they stood (Rom. 5:2). *It had required the work of the cross to put them there.* They were, however, being seduced away from the place Christ had gained for them by His death on the cross. For He "gave Himself for our sins that He might deliver us from (or *out of*) *this present evil world."* They were being persuaded to return again to it, and for a purpose (perfecting themselves in righteousness) which denied the effectiveness of the work of the cross, and hence put dishonour upon Him Who suffered for us there.

We see then that, in the Epistle to the Galatians, the cross is viewed not as the place where our sins were long ago judged and punished in the Person of our Substitute, God's Holy Lamb, but AS THAT WHICH AT THE PRESENT TIME STANDS BETWEEN US AND THE WORLD AND ITS WAYS, PARTICULARLY ITS RELIGIOUS WAYS. Here we see the cross, not only as taking away our sins, but as *separating us from the world.* Such is the import of those remarkable words: "I have been crucified with Christ" (2:20, R. V.). Such is the import also of the reason Paul gave for glorying in the cross of our Lord Jesus Christ, which was—not that expiation was there made for his sins, but that thereby *the world,* with its bad things and its good things, was crucified to him and he to the world (6:14).

Moreover, the Galatians, in following the false teaching which Paul denounces in this Epistle, would have abandoned *the proper life of sons of God* (as marked out for them in the words and commandments of the Lord) and would have exchanged it for the "bondage" of a life of religious routine. This explains the relation of the special subject of "liberty" and "bondage" (into which we purpose to inquire further in what follows) with the theme of the Epistle as a whole.

Finally, in connection with the results of the Lord's sufferings and death for us upon the cross, prominence is given here, and in the New Testament Scriptures generally, to the coming of the Holy Spirit of God, and His abiding presence with the saints. This dispensation is, in fact, the dispensation of the Holy Spirit. It was announced by John the Baptist in the words "The Kingdom of heaven is at hand," and was specifically described by him when he proclaimed the Coming One as He Who should baptize with the Holy Ghost.

In order that the people of God should be perfected in holiness, should walk in the ways of God, should fulfil the law of Christ, should bring forth fruit unto God, it was *necessary that the Spirit of God should come down to dwell with and in them.* And in order that the Spirit might come down for these purposes it was *necessary* that Christ should first die, should rise again, and be glorified in heaven (John 7 : 39 ; 15 : 7). The professed object of that life of religious "bondage" into which the Galatians were being enticed was to accomplish *by other means,* what the Holy Spirit had come to accomplish in and through the saints, namely, to perfect them in growth, and to make their lives fruitful to the praise of God. Hence the false teaching had the object of drawing them back, so to speak, into the previous dispensation—the dispensation before the Spirit was given—and in which rites and ceremonies, the observance of days and months and times and years, were appointed as types and shadows of the good things to come (Col. 2 : 17 ; Heb. 10 : 1). In the light of these facts it is easy to grasp the meaning of the question: "Are ye *so foolish?* having begun in the Spirit are ye now being *made perfect* in the flesh?" (3:3, Gr).

The subject of the Spirit's presence in the saints, and of His work in them and through them, comes very prominently into view in chapters 3, 4, and 5 of the Epistle we are studying; and we purpose giving it consideration later on.

III.

"THE TRUTH OF THE GOSPEL"

There is no need to dwell at length upon the historical incidents to which reference is made in chapters 1 and 2, since the bearing of those incidents upon the matters in hand is easily seen. We shall therefore give them but brief notice.

Paul refers to his "conversation in time past in the Jews' religion," or, in other words, to his manner of life in Judaism,* during which time he was devoting himself zealously to persecuting the Church of God and ravaging it. He was therefore thoroughly informed as to Judaism, and knew perfectly the antagonism between that system of legal bondage and the free church of God. He knew, too, that it had required a miracle of Christ's mighty power to deliver him from his blindness as a Jewish zealot, to bring him, like a little child, literally *led by the hand* (Acts 9:8), into the Kingdom of God's dear Son, and to make him willing to accept and obey commands brought by the very ones he had come to persecute at Damascus. Therefore he could clearly foresee the disaster that would fall upon the saints in Galatia if they should be enticed into the observance of Jewish rites.

This, of course, is not in anywise a reflection upon

---

*The word "religion" does not occur in this Epistle. It is found only in Acts. 26:5; and James 1:26, 27. Christianity is not a relgiion. Human religions are like costumes, prepared for special occasions, with Various trimmings for different seasons of the year. Christianity is a *life to be lived every day of the year,* a life which only they *can* live who have been born *of* the Spirit and are indwelt *by* the Spirit.

Judaism as originally established by God, and as it was
before it became corrupted through the traditions of men.
As originally established it was a marvellous witness to
the coming work and glories of Christ. It owed its entire value, however, to the fact that, in all its various and
elaborate details, it was "a shadow of *good things to
come."* For that very reason the actual coming of Christ,
and His fulfilment of those types and shadows, of necessity *abolished Judaism.* Therefore, to revive or to return to those fulfilled types and shadows was a slight
upon the work of Christ, and hence a grievous thing in the
eyes of God. It follows that it is a thing even more
grievous in God's eyes for His people to engage in religious observances of purely *human* origin. For if there
be now no place for Jewish ceremonial religion—its ritual,
priesthood, vestments, feasts, rites, etc.—how much less
is there place for any other? How grievous then in
God's sight must be the atrocious mixture of Jewish and
pagan liturgical arrangements and services, ceremonies,
vestments, sacerdotal orders, holy days and seasons
(largely derived from the idolatrous worship of the
heathen) to which modern Christendom is almost wholly
given over? The tendency to return to these things is
deeply rooted in the human heart; and there is need of
constant watchfulness against it.

Paul refers also to the fact that as a young man his
prospects in Judaism had been exceedingly bright, beyond those of others who were his equals in age, (1 : 14).
This is a further evidence that nothing short of the
mighty power of God could have changed him from the
chief persecutor of the church into its most efficient
apostle and minister.

Paul speaks of himself as having been "separated" to the service of God from his mother's womb. In Rom. 1 : 1 he says he was "separated unto the gospel of God." In Gal. 1 : 15, he adds: "from my mother's womb." In like manner God made known to Jeremiah that, before he was born, He had sanctified him (*i. e.,* had separated or set him apart) to be "a prophet unto the nations" (Jer. 1 :5). God foresees the service which His called ones are to perform. Jeremiah was to be "a *prophet* unto the nations" to pronounce God's judgments upon them; and Paul was to be an *apostle* unto the nations to bear to them the message of God's pardoning love in Christ Jesus. And both were selected for God's service from their mother's womb.

There is a widespread idea that Paul spent three years in the deserts of Arabia in preparation for his ministry. But what he distinctly says is that the three-year period referred to was *after* he returned from Arabia to Damascus. This is the statement: "I went into Arabia, and returned again unto Damascus. *Then* after three years I went up to Jerusalem to see Peter, and abode with him fifteen days" (1 : 17, 18).

This first visit of Paul to Jerusalem after his conversion is described in Acts 9 : 26-30. It was preceded by a period of active and effective witnessing in Damascus. His second visit, after a further interval of fourteen years, was the momentous occasion when he went "by revelation" (Gal. 2 : 2), accompanied by Barnabas, Titus and others, to bring before the apostles and the church at Jerusalem the great question whether converts from among the Gentiles should be circumcised and taught to keep the law of Moses. A full account of this event is given in Acts 15. Referring to this visit, Paul points out (in writing to the Galatians) that not even Titus, being a Greek, was compelled to be circumcised. In order to get the sense of this passage it is needful to observe that verse 3 is parenthetical, and that verse 4 continues the recital begun in verse 2. The sense is this: "I went up by revelation, and communicated to them that gospel which I preach among the Gentiles. And the reason for my going up to Jerusalem was that false brethren, stealthily brought in, had come among us to spy out our liberty in Christ," etc. That is to say, the reason why Paul went up to Jerusalem and communicated to the apostles the substance of what he was preaching among the Gentiles, was because of the coming of those referred to as "false brethren," who had come in among them by stealth to spy out the freedom which the saints enjoyed in Christ Jesus, and to contrive to bring them again into "bondage." Those "false brethren" are referred to in Acts 15:1, as "certain men which came down from Judea" to Antioch, and who "taught the brethren and said, 'Except ye be circumcised after the manner of Moses, ye cannot be saved.'"

What was involved in this attempt to seduce believers in the Lord Jesus Christ away from "the truth of the gospel" is forcibly declared by Paul's words in Gal. 5:2-4:

> "Behold, I Paul say unto you, that if ye be circumcised, Christ shall profit you nothing. For I testify again to every man that is circumcised, that he is a debtor to do the whole law. Christ is become of no

effect unto you, whosoever of you are (being) justified by the law; ye are fallen from grace."

We withhold our detailed comment upon this passage,
desiring at present only to point out that for believing
Gentiles to submit to circumcision as insisted upon by
the "false brethren" referred to, would have placed them
under obligation to observe the whole law of Moses, with
all its rites, ceremonies, sacrifices, offerings, feasts, and
other holy days and seasons. It would amount to a *complete abandonment* of the truth that a man is not justified
by doing the things appointed by the law, but solely by the
work of God, and upon the ground of the redemption
that is in Christ Jesus.

Paul mentions also the fact (Gal. 2:6-10) that upon
comparing his preaching with that of the other apostles,
it was found that he had the complete message of God,
insomuch that they could add nothing to what he had
already received of the Lord.

The fact that Paul was at pains to communicate the
gospel as preached by himself to the other apostles shows
that he fully recognized that they had the true gospel for
all the world in this dispensation, and that it would never
do for him to be preaching anything different. In fact,
he said he communicated his gospel to the other apostles
lest by any means he "should run, or had run, in vain."
Furthermore, his statement that they "in conference
added nothing to me"—that is to say they found nothing
lacking in his preaching—proves that he and they had
precisely the same gospel. Again, Paul, in writing to the
Corinthians, after first declaring the gospel which he had
preached and they had received, referred to the preaching
of the other apostles, and said: "Therefore, whether it

were I or they, so *we* preach, and so ye believed" (1 Cor. 15: 1-11). In other words, they all preached the same gospel.

It was also made evident to those at Jerusalem that Paul had been expressly chosen of the Lord for the apostleship to the Gentiles; for Paul says, "When they saw that the gospel of the uncircumcision was committed unto me, as the gospel of the circumcision was unto Peter * * they gave to me and Barnabas the right hands of fellowship; that we should go unto the heathen, and they unto the circumcision." With that perfect understanding they parted, taking up severally the labors entrusted to them.

Reference is next made to an event of great significance which took place during a subsequent visit of Peter to Antioch. It appears that, at first, Peter had walked according to *the truth of the one and only gospel;* but afterwards, through fear of some who came up from Jerusalem, he withdrew and separated himself from the Gentile believers.* This influenced other Jews to dissemble in like manner, insomuch that even Barnabas also, who had been chosen by the Holy Spirit to be Paul's companion in the ministry among the Gentiles, was carried away with them.

Paul describes this conduct of Peter, Barnabas and other believers, as walking "not uprightly according to the *truth* of the gospel" (2: 14). What then .was that "truth of the gospel" which was being set aside by the conduct of Peter and the others? It was nothing less than

---

*Showing how "the fear of man bringeth a snare" (Prov. 29:25).

the great fact, hidden during previous ages in the secret counsels of God, that *the fulness of Christ was for Gentiles equally with Jews.* It was that great and precious "mystery" of which Paul so often makes mention.

It is clear then that what was involved is a matter vital to Christianity. That, indeed, could be inferred from the unparalleled spectacle here presented of one apostle— the last and "least of the apostles"—administering severe rebuke (before all the company of saints) to another apostle, and he *the chief of them all.* Furthermore, from the fact that the extraordinary occurrence in question has been recorded by inspiration of the Holy Spirit for the instruction of the church throughout this age, we may gather assuredly that we have here a matter of permanent importance to the saints of God. Therefore we dwell for a while upon this strange happening, in order to get a clear idea of what was involved.

Many passages of Scripture declare that one effect of the death of Christ was the breaking down forevermore of the separating wall—"the middle wall of partition"— which God Himself had, in the preceding dispensation of "the law and the prophets," reared up between Jews and Gentiles. But the now revealed truth of the gospel, which previously had been a "mystery," is that Gentiles, who in the past dispensation were "afar off," are now in Christ Jesus, made nigh by His blood. We quote in this connection the words of Paul in Ephesians 2: 13-15, where, after referring to the state of the Gentiles in the past dispensation as aliens from the commonwealth of Israel, without Christ, without hope, and without God, he says:

"But now in Christ Jesus ye who sometimes were

far off are made nigh by the blood of Christ. **For** He is **our** peace"—that is, the peace or perfect oneness between believers from among Jews and Gentiles— "Who hath made both"—both Jews and Gentiles— *"one,* and hath broken down the middle wall of partition between us; having abolished in His flesh the enmity, even the law of commandments contained in ordinances"—which had been given to Jews but not to Gentiles—"for to make *in Himself* of twain (Jew and Gentile) one new man, so making peace" (that is, bringing into accord or oneness).

Enough appears by this one Scripture (out of many that bear on the subject) to show that Peter, Barnabas and the others who dissembled* "likewise" were setting aside the work of the Cross, reopening a breach which the Lord's death had closed, and were dividing the *one* body of Christ. It was a most serious matter surely.

This great "truth of the gospel"—namely, that "the unsearchable riches of Christ" were for Gentiles equally with Jews—which Paul had been specially called and commissioned to preach (Eph. 3:8), was *well known* to Peter and the rest. The Lord had plainly told His disciples, in explaining the parable of the wheat and tares (and doubtless on many other occasions, some of which are recorded), that the field in which the Word of the gospel was to be sown was not merely the land of Israel, but "the world." After His resurrection especially He spoke to them of "the things pertaining to the kingdom of God," and commanded them to go into *all the world,* to preach the gospel to *all creation,* and to disciple *all nations.*

Dissemble together—to act a feigned part or to act hypocritically in concert with others.

For He sent them not into Judea only, but "into *the world"*; and He charged them that repentance and remission of sins (the *gospel,* in a word) should be preached in His Name among all nations beginning at Jerusalem (Mat. 28:19, 20; Mark 16:15; John 17:18; Lu. 24:47).

Peter in particular had been instructed as to this "mystery."* In preaching on the day of Pentecost Peter had said that the promise of the Spirit, bestowed upon those who repent and believe. on the risen Christ, was given not only to the children of Israel, but also "to all them that are *afar off,* as many as the Lord our God shall call" (Acts 2:39). Also God had revealed "the mystery" to Peter by means of the vision of the great sheet let down from heaven (see Acts 10:9-16, and 28).

Peter had previously quoted the prophecy of Joel which foretold that *"Whosoever* shall call on the Name of the Lord shall be saved" (Acts 2:21). Furthermore. Peter had been, in a most remarkable way, prepared and commissioned to act upon this very "truth of the gospel," as recorded in the tenth chapter of Acts. That he well understood the lesson conveyed by the vision of the great sheet let down from heaven clearly appears by his words to the centurion Cornelius, when he entered the latter's house, thus associating himself with the abhorred "Gentile." To Cornelius and his company he said:

"Ye know how that it is an unlawful thing for a

---

*It is astonishing, in the light of such facts as those referred to in the text aboVe, that many should suppose "the mystery" to be the church, and that it was reVealed primarily to and through Paul; whereas the church was in Vigorous existence long .before Paul was conVerted, and it was *persecuted by him;* and moreoVer, "the mystery" is not the church, but the equal position of *Gentiles* with Jews in the church. In the "Scofield Reference Bible" it is stated that the church was "another 'mystery' *revealed through Paul"* (note on 1 Cor. 15: 24). For a correction of this error see the booklet "Paul and the Mystery," Hamilton Bros. 5c.

man that is a Jew to keep company or come unto one of another nation; but *God hath showed me that I should not call* ANY MAN COMMON OR UNCLEAN" (Acts 10:28).

Some years after this great event which in a formal and impressive way declared *the full equality of Gentiles with Jews for all the purposes of God's gospel of grace and pardoning love,* Peter himself set forth this "truth of the gospel" before the assembled apostles and elders and the "multitude" of believers gathered at Jerusalem, using these words:

> "Men and brethren, ye know that a good while ago God made choice among us, that *the Gentiles by my mouth* should hear *the Word of the Gospel* and believe. And God, Which knoweth the hearts, bare them witness, *giving them the Holy Ghost even as He did unto us;* and put *no difference between us and them,* purifying *their* hearts by faith" (Acts 15:7-9).

Notwithstanding this clear statement from the lips of the man who had been expressly chosen of God to carry out the truth under consideration, we find that same apostle, shortly thereafter, walking in direct contradiction to that very truth, and himself *putting a difference* where God had removed *all* difference, thus, in the language of Paul, building again the very things which God had, and that through Peter's own ministry, completely "destroyed."

There is much to learn from this incident. We have spoken already of the testimony it bears to the immense importance, in God's eyes, of that "truth of the gospel" upon which depends God's "eternal purpose which He purposed in Christ Jesus our Lord" (see Eph. 3:11, and verses precding). But it teaches also that even the servants of the Lord who have been most used of God may be found walking in ways that are contrary to the very truth they have clearly proclaimed. This lesson is *greatly needed in our day;* for often when some truth of the gospel is urged for the *obedience* of saints we are referred, as a reason for non-compliance, to the example of certain prominent leaders, it may be men whom God has gifted for His service and has even used in a conspicuous way, who nevertheless have chosen to walk in a broad and popular path, thus escaping in some measure "the offence of the cross" and "the reproach of Christ," or have otherwise failed in *"doing* the truth" (John 3:21; Gal. 3:1; 2 John 4; 3 John 3, 4).

Let us then give earnest heed to the fact that "the truth of the gospel" is a thing not merely to be committed to the memory, but to be manifested in all our walk and ways. And let us bear always in mind that we are to follow those who teach and minister the Word of God, only so far as they themselves walk in the truth thereof.

IV

"THE FAITH OF THE SON OF GOD"

The more closely Paul's words of reproof to Peter are examined, the more clearly it will be seen that the matter for which he was contending related to the way saints are to *live,* rather than to the way sinners are converted. Paul began by asking:

> "If thou, being a Jew, *livest* after the manner of Gentiles, and not as do the Jews, why compellest thou the Gentiles to live as do the Jews?"

Peter had, in obedience to the truth, abandoned the customs ("the law of commandments contained in ordinances") which God had imposed upon the Israelites in the preceding dispensation, but which the death of Christ had abolished. The abandonment by Peter, the leader of the apostles, of the custom of keeping apart from Gentiles and refusing to eat with them, was the strongest kind of witness to the fact that such customs had been abolished. But here he was, not merely returning to those observances himself, but actually compelling believers *from among the Gentiles* to submit to them, thus bringing *them* into bondage. This might seem to some a small matter. But what was back of it was the great question of the perfecting of the saints of God. This appears by the words ˈwhich follow:

> "We who are Jews by nature, and not sinners of the Gentiles—knowing that a man is not justified by

the works of the law but by the faith of Jesus Christ
—*even we* have believed in Jesus Christ that we
might be justified by the faith of Christ, and not by
the works of the law, for by the works of the law
shall no flesh"—whether Jew or Gentile—"be
justified."

In order to gain a clear understanding of this passage
it is necessary to bear in mind that the word "justification" means something more than the act of clearing a
man of his past sins when he comes to Christ.   That is,
indeed, its primary and usual meaning.   But it has also
the broader meaning of the *continuing* work of God in
the converted man during his life in the world.   The
words of chapter 2: 17—"if while we *seek to be* justified
by Christ"—and those of chapter 5, verse 4—"whosoever
of you are *being justified* by the law"—together with the
effect of the above quoted passage as a whole, show that it
is in this sense of a *continuing work of God* that the
word is here used.   With this understanding the meaning
of the passage is quite clear.   There could be but one
purpose for which a saint of God would resort to the
abolished Jewish observances, and that would be to *perfect himself in holiness,* to keep from defilement and con-
tamination through avoiding contact with that which is
unclean (in the case of not eating with Gentiles), or to
sanctify oneself (in the case of submitting to circumcision or of observing holy days and seasons).   The saint
who did such things would be taking the work of justifi
cation out of God's hands into his own, and would be de
pending for his spirtiual growth upon vain religious works
of men, instead of upon the merits of Christ's work and

the operation of the Holy Spirit of God in the believer's heart and life.

We learn then, through these words of Paul, that we are just as dependent upon the work of God, through Christ and the Holy Spirit, for our complete justification, or in other words for our "being made perfect" (3:3), as we were dependent upon His work for our regeneration. Whether, therefore, it be the *giving* of the life in Christ, or the *living* of that life, it is *by the power of God alone* that the desired result is attained. We are just as helpless, so far as our own efforts avail, for the work of perfecting ourselves in Christ, as we were for the work of quickening ourselves when we were dead in trespasses and sins. This is a great truth to lay hold of; but it is to its *practical* bearing and value that we wish to call special attention. We hope also to show in a subsequent chapter how this truth is illustrated and enforced in the allegory of Galatians 4:22-31.

What then is *our* part in the carrying on to perfection (or completion) of that work which God began in us when He gave us the new birth, sending forth the Spirit of His Son into our hearts, whereby we cry "Abba, Father"?—or (as it is put in Romans 5:5) when He "shed abroad His love in our hearts by the Holy Ghost Who is given to us"? The answer is found in the twice repeated words of verse 16 (quoted above): "Not by the works of the law, but *by the faith of Jesus Christ,*" "that we might be justified *by the faith of Christ,* and not by the works of the law."

Briefly then, our part is BELIEVING GOD. For just as in our conversion, what we had to do was to believe God, so in our being made perfect, our part is still to believe Him. All that is involved in "believing God" is not, indeed, apparent at the first glance; but we count upon help from the sanctuary to give our readers some little understanding of it at least. It is needful, however, to establish clearly that the part allotted to us in the accomplishing of God's purpose in us is *faith* from beginning to end. In addition, therefore, to the words of verse 16, which show "the faith of Jesus Christ" as the path to complete justification, we call attention to the familiar words of verse 20: "And the life which I *now live in the flesh* I live *by the faith of the Son of God.*"

These words fully support our statement. Paul is speaking of the life *he was living at that time* as a saint of God *"in the flesh,"* comparing it with the life *they* were living who were seeking to justify themselves by legal religious works. So strongly does Paul wish to assert the truth that the living of his life to the purposed end of full justification was altogether a supernatural thing—the power of Christ—that he counts himself as one dead—"crucified with Christ"—and says it was really not himself that lived but Christ Who was living in him.

This verse (Gal. 2:20) not only establishes that our part in the completion of God's work in us is *faith,* but it shows that the faith required of us is *not a passive thing,* a mere attitude of the mind, a mere mental acquiescence in what God has said—which is seemingly all that is meant by "faith" to many in our day. Such faith as that is altogether useless. It is not *faith* at all. Some of the great Bible words, such as faith, belief, grace, repentance, salvation, have been emptied of their meaning until only the shell—the mere outer form or sound of the word—remains. And this suits very well the temper and disposition of an easy-going, self-indulgent, pleasure-loving age.

But the faith whereof the apostle spoke was a thing of ceaseless activity. He lived by it. Such is real Bible-faith. In chapter 5, verse 6, it is spoken of as a *working* faith—"faith which *worketh* by love." What character-ized the men of faith whose names are enrolled in the eleventh chapter of Hebrews is not that they believed in a passive way that what God had said was true, but that their whole *course of action,* their entire path through the world, was shaped by the Word of God, insomuch that their lives, their conduct, their decisions, their ocen-pations, were altogether different and even contrary to what they would have been had God's Word not been heard and heeded by them. How is it with the one who writes and with those who read these lines? Have we, by definite choice, committed the whole course of our lives with all their interests, incidents, relationships, pur-suits, objects, satisfactions—all that comes within the compass of our daily existence—to the complete control of the revealed will of God? Have we, in sincerity and truth, before God and before men, taken the position of being crucified with Christ to all the influences and attrac-tions of this present evil world, giving ourselves over to our Lord and Saviour to be His absolute property, so that He may live His own life in us, and may express Himself through us to others—in love to the brethren, in compassion and kindness to the unconverted? This, we understand, is what it means to live by the faith of the

Son of God. It is a resurrection-life in a sense; for it is a life found only where death has wrought—even *the death of the cross.* For Paul first testifies that he has been "crucified with Christ" before he speaks of living that life which in reality was not himself but Christ living in him. Nor is it hard to see the truth of this in the records we have of that servant of Christ. We can readily picture the manner of life of Saul of Tarsus during the period when he gloried in his religious heritage and in his personal rectitude and morality, when from his youth (as he declared to Herod Agrippa) after the most straitest sect of Judaism he lived a Pharisee; and when his religious zeal expressed itself in making havoc of the church, committing both men and women to prison, breathing out threatenings and slaughter against the disciples of the Lord, and persecuting them even to distant cities. That man was dead. Through the law he died to the law. When and how was that? It took place when the light of God's truth burst upon him, showing him that, for all his religion, morality and self-righteousness, he was a sinner cursed by the law.

The sentence of death had been righteously passed upon him. But, by a miracle of God's grace and power, the execution of that judgment had been forever arrested. Why? Because Another, even the Son of God Who loved him and gave Himself for him, had been put to death in his stead. The curse which he deserved had fallen upon the Righteous One. It had been revealed to Paul, in that flood of light within his spirit, corresponding to the light above the brightness of the sun which had smitten him blinded to the ground, that "Christ hath re-

deemed us from the curse of the law, being made a curse
for us; for it is written, Cursed is every one that hangeth
on a tree" (3:13). And finally he saw that, in Christ's
death upon the tree, *he himself* had died. As he says in
another place :"For the love of Christ constraineth us;
because we thus judge, that if One died for all, then were
all dead" (2 Cor. 5:14). Therefore, *by faith* Paul reck
oned himself to be dead indeed unto sin, but alive unto
God in Christ Jesus. So Paul was crucified, in his own
consciousness and by the reckoning of faith. Not only
so, but it is recorded that "he was *three days* without
sight, and neither did eat nor drink" (Acts 9:9). However, after those three days of death and burial, he, like
the One Whom he was to serve all his days on earth and
to praise through the endless days of eternity, came to
life again—but as a *new man*. His first act was to be
baptized, calling on the Name of the Lord (in other
words confessing Christ as Lord), thus accepting the sign
of death and burial with Christ; and only after that did
he partake of food. It was not the same man that came
to life after those three days of death and darkness. It
was a new man, who not only had received new life in
Christ, but who was thenceforth to "walk in newness of
life." For Paul exemplified in his walk and ways the
truth of his words to the Galatians: "For as many of you
as have been baptized unto Christ have *put on Christ*"
(3:27).

Let us not miss the significance of the fact that the life
which Paul was living by the faith of the Son of God was
that which, in his own words, "I *now* live in the flesh." It
is only "now," and "in the flesh" that this life of faith

can be lived.   What an opportunity to glorify God, and bring forth fruit unto His praise is thus offered to us! Let us not neglect it.   Saul of Tarsus was, by nature, of precisely the same stock as we ourselves, for he himself says: "I am as ye are" (4:12) ; and the grace of God that turned him into Paul the apostle is available to us equally as it was to him.   The love of Christ is the same toward us as it was toward that persecutor of the church, the chief of sinners ; and the Holy Spirit is just as mighty to work in and through the least of God's saints today as He was at that time.   What then is lacking?   Is not the lacking thing indicated by the question which the Lord once put to His disciples: "Where is your *faith?*"

V

DEAD TO THE LAW

"For I through the law am dead to the law, that I might live unto God" (Gal. 2:19).

It is very desirable that we should know just what meaning is to be given to the words "dead to the law"; for here again man's natural desire to be free from all control and restraint, and to refuse everything that interferes with the doing of his own will, makes it fatally easy for him to accept the idea that "dead to the law" means there is no law he is bound to obey. The words quoted are far from conveying that meaning, nor is there anything in the Scriptures to support it. On the contrary, those who are saved by grace and redeemed by the blood of Christ, have a far greater obligation as regards obedience to the Word of God than ever rested upon Israelites in the flesh. Let us then be on our guard against the idea that the believer in Christ is dead to *the law of God;* for that is exactly what he has been *made alive to.* The mind of the flesh "is not subject to the law of God, neither indeed can be" (Rom. 8:7). Therefore a man *must be born again* ere he can be subject to the law of God; and this is but another way of saying that "except a man be born of water and of the Spirit, he cannot enter into the Kingdom of God" (John 3:5). For to be in the *Kingdom* of God means to be subject to the *law* of God. The believer is, however, delivered through the death of Christ

from that "yoke of bondage" wherein a man was required to attain unto righteousuess (in other words to
be justified) by the doing of those things required by the
law, including the whole system of sacrifices, ceremonies,
observances of sacred days and seasons, and the like.
Peter speaks of the rites and ceremonial observances of
the law as "a yoke * * which neither our fathers nor
we were able to bear" (Acts 15:10). And Paul speaks
of these *works* of law as "the yoke of bondage" (Gal.
5:1).

The truth of the gospel in this regard is clearly set
forth in Romans 9:30-10:11, which shows the great difference between being under the law and being saved by
faith in Christ; and an attentive reading of that passage
wi'l no doubt enlighten such as are desirous of knowing
God's mind on this subject. We will endeavor to give
the substance of it in simple words. In the preceding
dispensation, that of the law and the prophets, Gentiles,
having been left to themselves without either law or gospel, did not follow after righteousness. But now they
(that is, those among them who have believed) have attained to righteousness, even the righteousness which is
of faith. But Israel (all except the believing remnant
referred to in the preceding verses of Romans 9) which
followed after a *law* of righteousness, did not attain
thereto. Why not? Because they sought it not *by faith*,
but as it were by *works of law.*

We see then, in this passage of Scripture, two roads
leading to "righteousness," one by faith in Christ, the
other by works of law. The man who chooses the "faith"
road attains his desired end, because he receives as a *gift*
(in other words "*by grace*") the benefit of Christ's work,

referred to in the words of verse 28: "For He will finish
the work and *cut it short in righteousness;* because a
short work will the Lord make upon the earth." But the
man who chooses the long road of "works of law," never
attains unto righteousness, because he is *utterly unable to
do the necessary works.* Hence Paul's lament concerning
the Israelites of his day was that, being ignorant of *God's*
righteousness (attained by faith) and setting about to
establish *their own* righteousness (by works of law), they
had not submitted themselves unto the righteousness of
God. For Christ is the end of the law for (or unto)
righteousness (in other words the end aimed at through
the works of law) for everyone that believeth. Then follows a contrast between the law promulgated through
Moses, and "the word of faith" preached by Paul. This
requires no explanation.

The believer, then, enjoys, through the death of Christ,
perfect deliverance from "the yoke" of the law, that is
from all effort at the attainment of righteousness by the
doing of "works of law." In that sense he is "dead to the
law." The thought is that his effort as a natural man to
attain righteousness through doing all the things appointed
by the law ("continuing *in all things which are written
in the book of the law to do them*") was a failure. Hence
the law condemned him—it could not do otherwise—
and his life was forfeited. But, by the amazing grace of
God, the death of His own Son *paid the forfeit.* Hence,
in Christ, the believer is not only *freed* from the law,
but is actually counted as having *died* to it. This is the
sense of Paul's words: "For I through the law am dead
to (lit, died to) the law."

But let us carefully notice the next words—"*that I*

might live unto God." And now the question is, what sort of a life is this into which the believer is brought? Is it a life apart from the law of God? Quite the contrary—the very essence of it is the *fulfilling* of the law. But is the believer any more able than in his unconverted days to keep the law of God? In himself not a bit more able (and this fact is, we believe, the very heart of the lesson of Galatians as brought out clearly in the great allegory of chapter 4); *but God can now fulfil the law in him, through the Spirit dwelling in him.* This is strongly stated in the words: "Yet not I, but *Christ liveth in me";* and that life, insofar as it is Christ living in us, is a life of *perfect obedience to the law of God.*

This is so important that we would seek further to explain it by reference to the seventh chapter of Romans. The illustration of the relations of the wife to her husband is very illuminating if understood and rightly applied. For this we need only to observe the point of the illustration, which is, that as a consequence of the death of her husband, the woman is loosed, not from his person only, but from his *control*—"the *law* of the husband." The husband is plainly our old natural self, called in chapter 6:6, "our old man," now regarded as "crucified with Him" (Christ). Those words unmistakably connect the verse with Galatians 2:20. The woman who survives is our real self or personality, which is renewed and lives on in Christ. For a man's identity or conscious personality is not destroyed by his conversion. It remains and lives on in vital union with Christ. It is like the case of a woman whose husband dies, and who marries again. The woman is the same. But her life and her relations, duties, etc., as a wife, are totally changed. The *real* self or personality is

called in Romans 7 "the mind" (*nous* or conscious personality)—"I myself" (7:25).

With these facts clearly grasped the interpretation of the
parable becomes quite simple. If, however, the first husband is taken to be the law (which does not die, of course)
then hopeless confusion cannot be avoided.*

The truth then, which is set forth in Romans 7, is our
release from all the authority or control ("law") of our
old self, which release is effected by the death of Christ,
accounted or "reckoned" as the death of "our old man."

Paul, in presenting this illustration, says: "Know ye
not, brethren, for I speak *to them that know law.*" For he
does not say "know *the* law," which might mean the law
of Moses; but "them that know *law*" in general, meaning those who understand that the law has control of a
man only so long as he lives.

The object of law, as viewed in this passage (Rom.
6:21-7:4), is to produce in those under its control the
conduct, behaviour or manner of life—the doing of certain things and the not doing of certain other things—
that are in accordance with the commandments of the
law. The actions which the law of God seeks to produce in man are called in this and other passages "fruit."
But the law of the old man (the first husband), that is to
say the law by which we are all controlled in our natural
state, is "the law of sin and death." Paul had found
that law operating in himself, opposing and frustrating

---

*There is no question at all that the marginal reading of Rom. 7: 6 is
correct—"*we* being dead to that (the law) wherein we were held." Moreover, we *never were* joined as in marriage to the law; but were joined to
"our old man"; and hence the union was one which only death could dis-
solve. The law survives, and we are made alive again in Christ, to the end
(among other purposes of God) that the righteousness sought by the law
might be fulfilled in us.

his efforts to keep the law of God, as he said: "But I see *another law* (than the law of God) in my members, warring against the law of my mind, and bringing me into captivity to the law of sin" (Rom. 7:23, 25). Such is the "captivity" or "bondage" from which Christ, by His own death and by "the law of the Spirit of life" working within us, sets us free.

To the same effect Paul says in chapter 6:17, "Ye were the servants of sin," which is equivalent to saying: "Ye were under the law of sin." So he asks: "What *fruit had ye then in those things?"* (v. 21). The fruit of *that* law was, according to 7:5, "fruit unto death"; because "the end of those things is death" (6:21).

"BUT NOW" (6:22) how different!—"being MADE FREE FROM SIN," and having "BECOME SERVANTS TO GOD *ye have your fruit unto holiness"*! Attentive consideration should be given to this. In the words "made free from sin" we see a reference to "our liberty in Christ;" and this is declared also in the words: "For sin shall not *have dominion* over you; for ye are *not under the law* but *under grace"* (6:14). But we wish to call attention specially to the words "having become bondservants to God" (Gr.) This proves in the clearest way that our deliverance from the law of sin brings us into *complete subjection*—expressed by the strong word "bondservants"—*to the law of God.* Furthermore, it is to be observed that the new service is one which results in fruit—"ye have your fruit." Thus we arrive again at the conclusion already stated that by our conversion we are made, not dead to the law of God, but *alive* to it, and that we receive moreover power to fulfil it.

We are not now considering *how* the fruit is produced, or in other words how the life of the believer is made fruitful, but are seeking merely to make as plain as possible the fact that our life in Christ is a life wholly subject to the authority or "law" of God, to which the natural man is not subject, "neither indeed can be."

It is for the purpose of illustrating this truth concerning law, or authority, or control over the actions of men, that Paul refers as an illustration to the husband's authority over his wife and the wife's subjection to her husband. The points of this lesson are these: First, the wife is subject to the *law* of her husband; "bound" to him in law;* second, her subjection lasts only so long as the husband lives; hence if the husband should die she is "FREE FROM THAT LAW," that is from the law or control of the husband; and moreover she *may be married to another*.

And the simple application of the lesson is this: we who believe in *Jesus* Christ are made dead to the law, *i.e* ., the control or authority of "our old man," through the body of Christ, to the end that we may be united, as by marriage, to Another, even to Him who is raised from the dead; and this is for the purpose that "we should bring forth fruit unto God." Fruit is God's portion, and the bringing forth of fruit unto Himself is the end for which He deals with His people. Carrying the thought of law or authority into this last-cited verse (Rom. 7:4), we have the reminder that our relationship with Christ in resurrection, Who is Head of the body the Church, is

---

*The literal rendering of the first part of 7:2 would be, "For the married woman to the livng husband is bound in law"; the prominent thought of the whole passage being the subjection of the wife to the husband's *authority*.

like that of a wife with her husband in that we are subject to Christ. As it is written: "Therefore, as the
church is *subject unto Christ,* so let the wives be to their
own husbands in everything"(Eph. 5:24).

Briefly, then, in accepting salvation in Christ by faith,
we have passed from the authority (law) of the old man
to that of the New Man—Him Who was raised from the
dead "for our justification."

We will appreciate better the force of the illustration if
we bear in mind that marriage is, so to speak, the *joint*
life of two distinct individuals, a life which neither can
live alone; and that the "fruit" of marriage—children—
cannot be produced by one alone. Looking at the matter in
this light, we see that our former lives, which were lived
apart from Christ and *unto ourselves* (2 Cor. 5:15),
were barren and unfruitful towards God; for all the
"fruit" we produced, was "unto death."   But now, being
joined to another husband, even Christ "raised from the
dead," there is the possibility of our producing fruit *unto
God.*

We reach now the questions, What fruit are we to
bring forth? and how?

Romans 8:2-4, gives a clear answer to both questions.
(1) The "fruit" consists in *the very same righteousness
which the law required,* that is to say, the righteous acts
commanded by the law.   (2) This fruit is produced in
and through us by the operation of *"the law* of the Spirit
of life in Christ Jesus," displacing *"the law* of sin and
death."

Again, we would ask, Are we then any better able to
keep the law of God and to bring forth fruit unto God
after conversion than before?   Again we answer, in

ourselves, no. What makes the difference? The difference is *the Holy Spirit of God given to, and dwelling in the believer*. The presence and power of the Spirit of God changes everything so far as concerns living for God, bearing before men the testimony of a godly life, and bringing forth fruit to the praise of God.

It will be seen that, in the order of the unfolding of truth both in Romans and Galatians, we have first a strong assertion of the impossibility of a man being justified by works of law; then the death of Christ is brought in as *putting an end* to the old man and all his efforts at righteousness; then the new birth is referred to as *sonship* in the family of God, and as *new life* in the risen Christ; and, in connection with this new existence, *the Holy Spirit is revealed as given to the children of God to be the Power for that life.*

In Romans 8 we have a statement of many ministries which the Spirit performs for the children of God, with and in whom He abides. But here we wish to call attention only to the fact that the first purpose of all, announced in connection with the sending forth of God's own Son and the coming of the Spirit of life, is *"That the righteousness of the law might be fulfilled in us* who walk not after the flesh but after the Spirit."

Let it be noted that these words speak not of *our* fulfilling the righteousness required by the law, but of its *being "fulfilled* in us"; showing that the fulfilment is really *the work of Another* in us, even that of God the Holy Spirit. It is seen at a glance that this is in perfect agreement with Paul's words in Galatians 2:20: "I live, yet not I, but Christ liveth in me." It is Christ then Who lives in us by the Spirit. In Romans 8:9-10 the truth in this regard (which, since it involves the Being of God the Father, Son and Holy Spirit, is too vast for us to comprehend) is stated thus:

"But ye are not in the flesh, but in the Spirit, if so be that the *Spirit of God* dwell in you. Now if any man have not the Spirit of Christ, he is none of His (lit., not of Him). And if *Christ be in you,* the body is dead because of sin, but the *Spirit is life* because of righteousness."

It is clear that the various expressions "Christ in you," "the Spirit of God dwell in you," "have not the Spirit of Christ," are the same in significance, meaning that God (or Christ) dwells in the believer in the Person of the Holy Spirit.

In Galatians mention is made, as in Romans 8:2, of fulfilling "the law of Christ" (Gal. 6:2); and the law of Christ is, of course, all things that Christ our Lord has commanded. Paul is here carrying out the great commission (Mat. 28:19, 20). He had made disciples out of the mixed nations of Galatia: those disciples had been baptized; and now he was teaching them the things commanded by Christ—"all things whatsoever I have commanded you"; and, moreover, Christ was with him in this service, as He had promised. So in this connection we should recall that, in the Sermon on the Mount, which contains "the law of Christ," He expressly said: "Think not that I am come to destroy the law and the prophets: I am not come to destroy but *to fulfil*" (Mat. 5:17). He thereupon instructs His disciples how to be *perfect in love* (Mat. 5:43-48). This is repeated by Paul in Romans 13:8-10, where we find the words: "Owe no man anything but *to love one another;* for he that loveth another has fulfilled the law"; and also in Galatians in the words: *"By love* serve one another; for all the law is fulfilled in one word, even in this; Thou shalt love thy neighbour as thyself" (5: 13, 14).

Such is "the simplicity that is in Christ" (2 Cor. 11: 3) that the law as given by Him to the household of faith is all contained in "one word"—LOVE. And furthermore, the keeping of the law on their part is not a matter of the routine observance of fixed rules written in statute books or graven upon tablets of stone, but the very different matter of living out the life of Christ according to the love of God shed abroad in our hearts by the Holy Ghost Who is given to us.

The keeping of the law of God is simply the doing of the will of God; and the will of God is simply the expression of what God is; and "God is Love." Hence to be perfect in love, "which is the bond of perfectness," is to be perfect in life and conduct. For if a man love his neighbour there is no need to tell him not to kill him, nor steal from him, nor slander him, nor covet his possessions. Hence "love is the fulfilling of the law."

THE LAW OF CHRIST

What, then, is "the law of Christ" which they who have been quickened from their natural state of death in sins are called to obey? What does it embrace, and what does it not embrace, of the commandments of God found in the Bible? It is of the utmost importance that we should have a clear understanding as to this. Let us therefore seek it diligently, counting upon the help of the Holy Spirit Who desires that we be filled with the knowledge of God's will in all wisdom and spiritual understanding (Col. 1:9).

Discernment and discrimination are needed here, since evidently not *all* of God's commandments found in the Bible are for His people of this dispensation. Under the old covenant God chose the children of Jacob to be His people, and to them He gave a law with "statutes and judgments" which they were to keep. But, under the new covenant, God has chosen as His peculiar people all those out of all the nations and tribes of the earth who, through the gospel, believe in Jesus Christ His Son. To them there has been no formal promulgation of law, as such. In fact, the word "doctrine" or "teaching" is more often used in this connection than the word "law." Obviously the word "doctrine" is more in keeping than the word "law" with the relations into which God has brought His new covenant people. They being His own children, He gives them "teaching" rather than "law." God's Word has, of course, the same binding force whether called by one name or by the other. One of the great differences between the old covenant and the new is indicated by the contrast between the word "servants" or "bondslaves" and the word "children." For the old covenant from Mount Sinai gendereth to bondage; whereas the new covenant answers to Jerusalem that is above, which "is *free,* which is the mother of us all" (Gal. 4: 24-26).

At Mount Sinai the ten commandments were spoken by the Lord in the hearing of all the people (Ex. 20), and they were also written on tables of stone. In addition, there were given certain "judgments" regulating the relations of the Israelites with one another (Ex. chaps. 21, 22, 23). Later God gave to Moses also the "ordinances" for worship; *i. e.,* directions for the tabernacle, its appointments, the priests, their garments, the manner of their consecration, etc. (Ex. chaps. 24 to 30 inclusive).

Inasmuch as God's mind and will in all matters pertaining to *the conduct* of men are unchanging, it is of necessity true that the law given on Mount Sinai stands forever as the expression of His will, except in those particulars wherein He Himself has repealed or modified it. Hence we find in "the doctrine of Christ" many of the same commandments that were given at Sinai. In fact, every one of the "ten commandments" is repeated in the New Testament *excepting the fourth.** It need hardly be said that all commandments which have to do with *what is right and wrong* must stand as God's inalterable requirement.

Looking closely, therefore, at the law in its completeness,

*See "Concerning the Sabbath," by Philip Mauro. 10c.

we can distinguish three kinds of commandments; *first,* those having to do with righteousness (called in Romans 8:4 "the righteousness of the law"); *second,* those having to do specially with "Israel after the flesh" (as, for example, the laws pertaining to their inheritance in the land of Canaan, their reciprocal duties as Israelites, their relations with the Moabites, Egyptians, and other neighbouring peoples, and the like); and *third,* the ordinances relating to "the service of God," that is to say to *worship.*

The third heading embraced a very large part of "the law," including many details concerning the tabernacle, the sacrifices, the priesthood, the keeping of feast-days and seasons, and the like. *All this part of the law has been fulfilled and is done away.* For this we have the clearest statements of the New Testament. Thus, in Hebrews 7:12, it is stated that "the priesthood being changed, there is made of necessity a change also of the law." And again (7:18, 19): "For there is verily a disannulling of the commandment going before, for the weakness and unprofitableness thereof. For the law made nothing perfect." The context shows clearly that what is here spoken of is that part of the law which has to do with the worship or service connected with the earthly Sanctuary, and which was committed to the family of Aaron as the priests of God. *Worship* is now transferred from earth to heaven; and the priesthood has been transferred from the house of Aaron to the house of Jesus Christ ("Whose house are we," Heb. 3:6). The Lord Jesus Himself spoke plainly of this important change then about to take place, saying to the woman of Samaria: "Woman, believe Me, the hour cometh when ye shall neither in this mountain *nor yet at Jerusalem* worship the Father. . . . But the hour cometh, and now is, when the true worshippers shall worship the Father in spirit and in truth; for the Father seeketh such to worship Him" (John 4:21-25). The repetition of the word "Father" in this saying of the Lord Jesus is important as declaring the character of the dispensation and of the Kingdom He was then about to introduce. It should be observed also that the interview with the woman of Samaria took place before the Lord began to preach in Galilee. He was *even then* declaring, not the setting up of David's throne at Jerusalem, but the complete aboli tion of the temple and of earthly worship there.

We are also distinctly told in Hebrews that "the first covenant had ordinances (*ceremonies*, marg.) of divine service, and a *worldly* sanctuary," and that the things pertaining thereto were "a figure *for the time then present*"; and also that "the service" consisted "only in meats and drinks, and divers washings, and *carnal ordinances,* imposed *until the time of reformation*" (lit. setting things right). "But Christ being come, an High Priest of good things to come"—those temporary arrangements are all set aside. (Heb. 9:1-11).

Paul refers in his Epistle to the Romans, to the same subject (of meats and drinks and the observing of days) as having no place in this present era; and it is instructive to note that, in this connection, he calls the present era the *Kingdom of God,* saying, "For the Kingdom of God is not *meat* and *drink;* but *righteousness* and peace and joy in the Holy Ghost" (Rom. 14:17).

All these "carnal ordinances" were but "a shadow of good things to come" (Heb. 10:1). Hence it is a serious error for us, who have the holy and eternal verities, whereof the law had only a shadow, to forsake the "good things" into which grace has brought us, and to take up again with the shadows. This is precisely the error into which the Galatians were being led, and concerning which the apostle asks: "Are ye so foolish? Having begun in the Spirit, are ye now being made perfect by the flesh?" (Gal. 3:3)—that is to say by rites and ceremonies, keeping of days, and other carnal (or fleshly) ordinances.

The sons of God, who have been re-born into the liberty wherewith Christ makes free, have nothing to do with those, or with any other ordinances or religious observances. The "shadows" of the Mosaic law are nevertheless of great value and interest to them, because they are *shadows of Christ and of His redeeming work—and of His ministries as the High Priest of the heavenly sanctuary.*

As regards that part of the law which pertained to the relations of Israelites with one another, and with the peoples of the world around them, it is obvious that those special "statutes and judgments" have no immediate or direct application to the children of God. Statutes relating to the redemption of land, the treatment of slaves, the incidents of the year of Jubilee, and the like, pertain to an earthly people. Nevertheless, there is instruction of much value to us in all these statutes and judgments: "For *whatsoever things* were written aforetime were written for our learning (i. e., instruction), that we, through patience and comfort *of the Scriptures* might have hope" (Rom. 15:4). "*All Scripture* is given by inspiration of God, and is profitable for *doctrine,* for reproof, for correction, for instruction in righteousness;

that the man of God may be *perfect,* thoroughly **fur-nished** unto *all good works"* (2 Tim. 3:16, 17).

The production of "good works" is, as we have seen, the aim of God's dealings with His people; and to that end *all* the Scriptures, if studied with a subject mind and a willingness to do the will of God, are "profitable."

The word "doctrine" (or teaching) has, in modern usage, a meaning radically different to that which it has in the Bible; and this should be clearly understood. There-fore we ask careful attention to the scriptural meaning of this word. This appears clearly by the first occurrence of the word. In giving commands to Moses God said· "Now therefore go, and I will be with thy mouth, and *teach thee what thou shalt say"* (Ex. 4:10). Teaching then consists in directions what to *do* and how to do it. A clear illustration is found in Exodus 18:20, where Jethro, speaking to Moses, said: "And thou shalt *teach them ordinances and laws,* and shalt show them the way wherein they must walk, and the work they must do." Again, in Exodus 24:12, we read: "And the Lord said unto Moses, Come up to Me in the mount and be there; and I will give thee tables of stone, and a law and com-mandments which I have written, that thou mayest *teach them."* And so Moses did; for when about to depart from the world he said: "Behold, I have *taught you statutes and judgments,* even as the Lord my God com-manded me, that ye should *do so* in the land whither ye go to possess it. Keep therefore and *do* them, for this is your *wisdom* and your understanding in the sight of the nations" (Deut. 4:5, 6). And he also commanded the Israelites to *"teach* them thy sons and thy son's sons,"

thus reminding them of what the Lord had said at Horeb:
"And I will make them hear My words, that they may
learn to fear Me all the days that they shall live upon the
earth, and that they may *teach their children*" (Deut. 4:
9, 10).

The usage of the word "doctrine" is the same in the
New Testament, as could be shown by a great many passages. A few however will suffice.

One of the most important passages in the Bible is the
sixth chapter of Romans, the burden of which is that
those who have been justified through the blood of Christ,
and have received eternal life, should yield themselves to
God for "OBEDIENCE UNTO RIGHTEOUSNESS" (Rom 6:
16). The apostle says: "But God be thanked, that ye
were the servants of sin, but ye have *obeyed from the
heart that form of doctrine which was delivered you.*
Being then *made free* from sin, ye became the servants of
righteousness."

The "form" or pattern of doctrine of which Paul
speaks is "the doctrine of Christ" (2 John 9, 10); and we
are here reminded again that it is to be "obeyed *from the
heart,*" that is to say, obeyed of our free will. Such is
the kingdom wherein grace reigns (Rom. 5:21).

To the same effect, in writing to the Corinthians Paul
promises to send to them Timothy, "Who," he says,
"shall bring you into remembrance of *my ways* which be
in Christ, as I *teach* everywhere in every church"; and in
this connection he adds the significant words: "For the
Kingdom of God is not in word, but in power" (1 Cor.
4: 17, 20).

In Titus 2:1-15 is a strong passage dealing with

"sound doctrine," and showing clearly what is meant by that expression (Comp. 1 Tim. 1:8-10). The same "grace of God that bringeth salvation" also *teaches us;* and the nature of the doctrine of grace (which is here called "the doctrine of God our Saviour") is that, "denying ungodliness and worldly lusts, we should *live soberly, righteously,* and *godly* in this present world." Thus it is that by obeying the commandments of Christ, we "adorn the *doctrine* of God our Saviour."

In John 7: 16, 17 the Lord Jesus made an important statement concerning His doctrine, saying: "My doctrine is not Mine but His that sent Me. If any man *will* do (that is, *desires or purposes* in his heart to do) His will, he shall know of the *doctrine,* whether it be of God, or whether I speak of Myself." From this it again appears that the doctrine of Christ is the Father's teaching (or commands), for His own children, imparted to them by the Son; and also that submission to His doctrine must be voluntary, even as His own obedience was voluntary. As He also said later to His deciples: "If ye keep My commandments ye shall abide in My love; even as I have kept My Father's commandments and abide in His love" (John 15: 10).

That which was the doctrine of the Father and the Son, became after Pentecost "the apostles' doctrine," they being instruments, indwelt by the Spirit of God, for communicating *teaching* to believers. And when the record says "they continued stedfastly in the apostles' *doctrine*" (Acts. 2:42), we are not to understand merely that they continued to hold orthodox views, but that they continned in the *doing* of the things taught by the apostles;

for they who are "hearers only" and not doers of the Word of the Lord "deceive their own selves" (Jas. 1: 22).

The doctrine of the Lord Jesus Christ, as given to us in the Gospels, is, of course, unchanged in the Epistles. The plain purpose of the latter is to unfold, expound and apply the Lord's own teaching—not to alter it.*

The beginning of the Lord's personal teaching is found in "the Sermon on the Mount," which is introduced by the words: "And He opened His mouth and TAUGHT them, saying" .... (Mat. 5:2). In this utterance—which is that of the Divine Legislator, imparting the Father's commandments to those whom He had given the right to become the children of God (John. 1:12), the Lord says at the outset: "Think not that I am come to destroy *the law* or *the prophets*. I am not come to destroy but to fulfil."

How then does He fulfil the law and the prophets? The true answer is (we believe) that He fulfils (or has already done so) the most important parts of both the law and the prophets *in His own Person;* and that He fulfils other parts *in His people* (who are yielded to His possession and authority) through the Spirit who dwells in them.

We have seen that the law embraced both ordinances of divine service (rites, ceremonies, offerings, etc.), and also things to be done "for righteousness' sake." The former (the ordinances, etc.) were all fulfilled in the Lord's sufferings, death and resurrection, except such as

*See "The Progress of Doctrine," by Bernard (Hamilton Bros.), a valuable and instructive work, which we heartily commend to all who are interested in the subject under discussion.

are now being fulfilled by Him as God's High Priest and the Advocate of His people.   The things to be done for righteousness' sake were likewise fulfilled by Him in Person, both as a Man and as an Israelite under law; but these requirements of the law are also being fulfilled by *Him in His people through the indwelling Spirit.*

So with the prophets.   Their predictions were in part fulfilled by His sufferings, death, resurrection and ascension to the throne of God.   But the *commandments* given by God through the prophets, so far as they have to do with righteous conduct, are being fulfilled in the people of God in this dispensation.   That part of the law and the prophets which remained for fulfilment in and through the saints of God is summed up concisely by the Lord in the familiar verse: "Therefore, all things whatsoever ye would that men should do to you, do ye even so to them; for *this is the law and the prophets.*"   To this also agrees His answer to the Pharisees when they asked Him which is the great commandment in the law.   His reply was briefly, Love to God with the whole being, and love for one's neighbor as for oneself; and He added the words: "On these two commandments hang *all the law and the prophets*" (Mat. 22:36-40).   Thus the substance of the law and the prophets is brought over unto this dispensation to be fulfilled, not by the people of God, but rather by God Himself *in* them.   And the substance of both the law and the prophets is expressed in the one word, *love.*

To the same effect are the words of Paul, who, in expounding the great subject of God's righteousness by faith, puts this pointed question: "Do we then *make void the law through faith?"* To which he gives the emphatic answer: "God forbid: yea, *we establish the law"* (Rom. 3:31).

In view of the instruction which by many teachers is being given to God's people in the present day, the truth declared by this question and answer is greatly needed: for the effect of that instruction is to "make void the law." But the truth is that the changed conditions brought about by the death and resurrection of Christ, and the coming of the Holy Spirit, served in reality to "establish the law," not to make it void; for it is only through re-born men, indwelt by the Spirit of God, that the law (as regards practical *righteousness,* or living soberly, righteously and godly in this present world) could be fulfilled.

In this same chapter Paul asks another question to which (and to the answer given by him) we should pay heed: "Where is boasting then? It is excluded. By what law? of works? Nay: but *by the law of faith"* (Rom. 3:27). We see then that faith also has its "law" but it is such as to exclude boasting. Why? Because, while a man would have whereof to boast if justified by his works, it is not so with those who are justified by faith, for it is God who works in them both to will and to do of His good pleasure.

In Romans Chapter 12-14 Paul gives certain commands which are embraced in the doctrine of Christ, and in these he virtually repeats the substance of the law, saying:

"Own no man anything but to love one another, for he that loveth another hath fulfilled the law. For this, Thou shalt not commit adultery, thou shalt not kill, thou shalt not steal, thou shalt not bear false witness, thou shalt not covet; and if there *be any other commandment,* it is briefly comprehended in this saying, Thou shalt love thy neighbor as thyself. Love worketh no ill to his neighbor: therefore love is *the fulfilling* of the law" (Rom. 13:8-10).

In the context we find also the following, which re-echoes the words of Christ in the Sermon on the Mount:

"Dearly beloved, avenge not yourselves, but rather give place unto wrath: for it is written, Vengeance is Mine; I will repay, saith the Lord. *Therefore,* if thine enemy hunger, feed him; if he thirst, give him drink; for in so doing thou shalt heap coals of fire on his head. Be not overcome of evil, but overcome evil with good" (Rom. 12:19-20).

Time and space would fail us should we attempt to set forth many specific instances in which the commandments of the law and the prophets are repeated in "the doctrine of Christ," given from His own lips and through His apostles. But enough has been said to show that "the law of Christ" embraces all "the law and the prophets" so far as these pertained to the *righteousness* which God requires of His people in their conduct.

There is one other matter that should be noted here. The Lord Jesus Christ, in proclaiming His doctrine in the Sermon on the Mount, transferred the action of the law, so to speak, from the region of the outward behavior to the region of the heart. He took the sixth commandment, which relates to a man's life, and the seventh, which relates to his wife, (the next most sacred thing), and enlarged their operation in such way as to forbid the *thought of the heart* from which the sinful act springs. This is deeply significant. It shows that, under grace, God purposes to have a people whose *hearts* are purified from evil thoughts and desires, and not merely a people whose outward behaviour is morally correct — for such were the Pharisees, and such was Saul of Tarsus in his unconverted days. God's purpose in taking us up in His grace is to conform us, by the working of the Spirit, to the image of His Son (Rom. 8:29; 2 Cor. 3:18). Our conformity with Christ must therefore begin *at the heart;* and the work of "the law of the Spirit of life in Christ Jesus" has not been fully accomplished until *every thought* has been brought into captivity to the *obedience of Christ.* (2 Cor. 10:5).

Therefore, when Paul said he lived by the faith of the Son of God, he meant that he lived by His *Word.* To live by *faith* in Christ is to keep the commandments of Christ; for faith cometh by hearing (which involves *obedient submission to what is heard*) and hearing by the Word of God. The life of faith is a life of *obedience;* and therefore the great requisites to such a life are *first,* love and devotion to the Lord Jesus Christ so that the desire to please Him shall be the ruling motive of our hearts, and *second,* that the Word of Christ should dwell richly within us. In the living of this life, that is to say, in the fulfilling of "the law of Christ," rites and ceremonies — even those given by God Himself to the Israelites — are worse than useless. "For in Jesus Christ neither circumcision availeth anything nor uncircumcision; but FAITH which WORKETH by LOVE" (Gal. 5:6). The faith that justifies is a faith which *works;* and moreover the power or energy in which the works are accomplished and their character-determined, is LOVE.

In bringing this chapter to a close we would point out the very significant fact that the false teachers against whom Paul raised so solemn a warning were not urging the Galatians to keep the *righteousness* of the law and the prophets, to love mercy, to do justly, to walk humbly, to give to the poor, to succour the fatherless and the widow, to forsake lying, stealing, covetousness, oppression, uncleanness, and every evil work; for those are the very things which are commanded in the doctrine of Christ and His apostles.   What those teachers of error were insisting upon was the observance of Mosaic rites, ceremonies and ordinances, which were but types and shadows pointing to the atoning work of Christ, and which were all abolished by His death on the cross.   And not only so, but they were insisting that the doing of such "works of law" was necessary to the complete justification of the saints of God.   Such teaching is, as we have seen, a denial of "the truth of the gospel;" for it detracts from the merits of the cross of Christ, it ignores the fact that believers in Christ are the born children of God, and it disregards the presence and work of the Holy Spirit.

VII.

THE PROMISE OF THE SPIRIT
(Gal. 3:14).

God's purpose in the call of Abraham was to procure for Himself a people answering fully to His own mind, and through them to bring "blessing" to all nations. Of Abraham God said: "I called him alone" (Isa. 51:2). Hence all the "called" of God must needs be the children of Abraham. But how is their relationship with Abraham to be reckoned? By natural descent or by spiritual descent? This deeply interesting question (truly of *vital* importance to Gentiles) is answered in the fourth chapter of Romans, and also in the third chapter of Galatians, which is now before us. The relationship is reckoned by spiritual descent: "For even as Abraham *believed God* and it was counted to him for righteousness," even so "they which are of faith," in other words they who like Abraham hear the word of God and do accordingly, "the same are the children of Abraham" (Gal. 3:6, 7).

What God requires in His people first of all is "righteousness," and this He purposes to have; for He declared, speaking of the heavenly Jerusalem, "Thy people shall be all righteous" (Isa. 60:21); and again: "This is the heritage of the servants of the Lord, and their righteousness is of Me, saith the Lord" (Isa. 54:17).

How then was this purpose of God to be accomplished? How could He obtain a "godly seed" (Mal. 2:15)? Could it be procured out of nature? Could it be produced by or from the flesh? Could the law of God, working through the flesh, and with the aid of religious observ- auces, rites and ceremonies, fasts and feasts, sacrifices and ordinances, yield the desired result? This question is not one of theoretical interest only, for God has given much space in His Word to the testing of the natural man with a view to making perfectly clear the facts of his condition, and the utter impossibility, *by any means whatever,* of reforming or rehabilitating the natural man to make him acceptable to God, or submissive to God's will, or serviceable for God's purposes. God has seen fit to make perfectly clear that, because of sin, the race of Adam is ruined past all possibility of recovery. He would have it demonstrated beyond all question that, in reject- ing the natural man, He is fully justified because of the impossibility of making him other than he is — corrupt and filled with all unrighteousness.

And not only has God given much space in His Word to the showing forth of man's true condition, but He has also appropriated many centuries of time to demonstrat- ing the impossibility of producing out of the race of Adam a single individual that could measure up, by his own efforts, to God's standard of righteousness. Such being the facts as to man's condition by nature, the *neces- sity* is proved of a *new creation-work of God.*

This is what we seek now, in humble dependence upon the enlightening power of the Holy Spirit, to look into; and it is evident that God would have us to do so, because He has been pleased to explain His plan and pur- pose in the Scriptures, giving many illustrations and helps to the understanding thereof. Thus, for the sake of affording us an object lesson, Abraham's family history was divided into two distinct parts; and likewise the history of his descendants — "Israel" — is divided into two corresponding parts. In Abraham's personal history we have the .period of his family-life with Hagar (there having been no family as the result of his marriage with Sarah); but the family resulting from that marriage would not answer the purposes of God, and was therefore rejected. Why? Because Ishmael was "born *after the flesh."* There was, therefore, in Abraham's life, *though he was a man of faith,* no "fruit unto God" until death had, so to speak, put an end to all that Abraham was by nature, and until no hope remained but through faith in God Who quickeneth the dead.

Likewise the history of the people of God. The nation Israel had first an Ishmael-period of activity in the flesh, during which time they enjoyed all the benefits and help of the law, and of a heavenly-given ritual of rites and ceremonies. But (though many individuals were saved *by faith* during that period) there was no "household of God," no family perfected in righteousness, bearing "fruit" for God, and giving a testimony for Him to the world.

God could and did send down the law from heaven by angels in the hand of a mediator. But, in order to secure for Himself a righteous people, He must *come down Himself,* and do a new work, finishing it and cutting it short *in righteousness,* whereby many might be "made righteous" (Rom. 5: 19). Something more was needed than a law from God in order to produce practical right-

eousness; and that something was "LIFE" That was
what the law could not produce through mankind;
"For, if there had been a law given that could have
given life, verily righteousness would have been *by the
law*" (Gal. 3:21). How then could a new *life,* uncor
rupted and uncorruptible, be imparted to dying men?
Only God could answer that question; and in marvellous
condescension He *has* answered it. For the accomplish
ment of that purpose there must be a *new Source of human life* in a *new Man,* One not tainted by the sin of
Adam. That much would be easy to understand; for
we can readily see that God could begin all over again
by the creation of another human race, with another head.
But the problem is far more complicated than that; for
what was purposed by God was that the new life was to be
given to those who had, through sin, forfeited their natural lives and merited eternal condemnation.

The new and perfect human race was to be built up
out of the spoiled material of the old. How could that
be done in righteousness? Clearly it was necessary that
complete satisfaction be made for all the sins of those to
whom the new life was to be given; and it was for this
that God sent forth His Son, made of a woman, made
under the law, to *redeem them that were under the law*
by dying in their stead upon the cross. This sacrifice of
Jesus Christ, Who was "made a curse for us," opened the
way for the promised "blessing of Abraham" to come
upon the Gentiles. And it is clear from the testimony
of all the Scriptures that there was no other way. The
precise nature of that promised "blessing" is not revealed
in the Old Testament. But we now know that what God

contemplated was the giving of eternal life through the imparting of the Eternal Spirit to those whom He purposed to call in His grace. To this we will return.

In the light of these facts it is not difficult to grasp the meaning of the passage before us. In the last verse of Chapter 2 Paul says: "I do not frustrate the grace of God; for if righteousness come by the law, then Christ is dead in vain" (literally "died for nought"). The grace of God provides righteousness as a "gift" to the believing sinner (Rom. 5:17). Hence, to seek righteousness through the observance of religious rites and ceremonies is to set aside, or to spurn, the grace of God. And the seriousness of the error for which Peter and others are here reproved, and against which the churches of Galatia were warned, appears from the fact that if righteousness were attainable by the law and by aid of the religious observances appointed for men in the flesh, then *Christ's death was needless.* A warning so solemn as this should surely suffice to keep the Lord's people from doing or taking part in any act that savors in the least of religious ceremonial, as for instance the observance of holy days and seasons, and the like. The danger of imitating the religious systems of christendom in their ever-increasing departure from the simplicity that is in Christ, especially in the matter of religious ceremonial — particularly the observance of days — is one against which the saints of God need to be continually on their guard. They may be wholly delivered by the truth of God from all thought of perfecting themselves in righteousness by such means; nevertheless we have to bear in mind the purpose for which such ceremonials and observances were instituted, and *what they really stand for.* And since their true significance makes the death of Christ a vain thing, we should *shun with horror* the very thought of anything in the nature of celebration of "Christmas," "Easter," and other festivals of pagan origin, which have been adopted by the corrupt churches of christendom. We should also be most careful to guard our children against this danger, and to teach them "the truth of the gospel" in this respect.

God gave to His people of old a warning concerning the nations He was about to cut off — a warning still needed by His saints — saying: "Take heed to thyself that thou be not ensnared *by following them* * * and that thou enquire not after their gods, saying, How did these nations serve their gods? Even so will I do likewise. * * Whatsoever thing I command you, observe to do it; thou shalt not *add* thereto, nor *diminish from it*" (Deut. 12: 30-32).

Paul bases his appeal to the Galatians on the fact that Christ had been set forth before their eyes in an evident way as *crucified,* that is to say, as having been put to death as a malefactor. In other words, he had clearly preached to them the effect of the cross in not only putting away their sins, but in bringing them into the grace of Christ, thus separating them from the world and all its systems of religion. He asks them therefore one pointed question, the answer to which would settle the matter in dispute·

"This only would I learn of you, *Received ye the Spirit* by the works of the law or by the hearing of faith?" (3:2).

Paul could safely rest the whole case on the answer

to that question; for he had himself been the channel of ministry through which they had received the Spirit (see verse 5); and he had of course instructed them in the truth that the Holy Spirit is the *Gift* of God, (Acts. 2·38; Rom. 5:5, etc.) bestowed on all those who hear and believe the gospel of Christ.*   Thus the apostle reminds them that they had "begun in the Spirit."   What they had begun was a *new life;* and the Holy Spirit had been given as the power for living that life into God, and bringing forth the fruit of it.   God has a *practical* object in view in all His dealings with men; and in this case the object is "fruit."   This figurative expression stands for those things brought forth in the lives of God's people which are a satisfaction to Him and a testimony to the world. Religious observances are not "the fruit of the Spirit;" for men in the flesh can engage in them just as heartily as converted persons.   Hence the point of the question, "Are ye so foolish?   Having begun in the Spirit are ye being perfected in the flesh?" (v. 3 Gr.)

The important thing then is the *perfecting* of the saints of God, that is to say their going on to full maturity in godliness and Christlikeness, and to the bringing forth of "fruit" to the praise of God.   And the important lesson here is that faith, or believing God, is ever and

---

*There is much confusion on this subject at the present time, because of erroneous teaching to the effect that the receiving of the Spirit is in the nature of a "second blessing," and that some efforts must be made —as praying, seeking, "consecrating oneself," or other human "works"—in order to obtain the Spirit. The teaching of Scripture is clearly to the contrary. The Spirit is *given,* as the Lord Himself promised, to them "that believe on Him" (John 7:39). In all the instances recorded in the New Testament there is none in which those who received the Gift of the Holy Spirit did anything but *believe the gospel.* The words "since ye believed," in Acts 19:2 and Eph. 1:13 should read *"when* ye believed," for those passages prove that the Spirit is received through the hearing of faith. The giving of the Holy Spirit to them that ask, of which the Lord spoke in Luke 11.13, was fulfilled at Pentecost, after the disciples had continued in prayer for ten days.

always that which is required on our part as the condition of God's work continuing in our hearts and lives.
Paul points to his own activity in the service of God, and
in that connection asks another pertinent question: "He
therefore" (meaning himself) "that ministereth to you
the Spirit and worketh miracles among you, doeth he it
by the works of the law, or the hearing of faith?" (v. 5).
We learn from this question that all the manifold activi
ties of the apostle's ministry, including even the working
of miracles, were by the hearing of faith; and if this be
sufficient for the life and labors of the great apostle of
the Gentiles, then surely the same rule applies to and will
suffice for all the people of God.

Paul next links his own rule of life with that of Abra
ham, saying: "Even as Abraham believed God, and it was
accounted to him for righteousness. Know ye, therefore, that they which are of faith, the same are the chil
dren of Abraham" (3:6, 7). The words "they that
are of faith" are significant. They show that the important thing for the purpose under consideration was not
a matter of having once believed in Jesus Christ and having received forgiveness of sins and the Gift of the Holy
Spirit, but a matter of *going on in the life of faith.*
"They that *are* of faith, the same are the children of Abraham;" and again in verse 9 we find the words "they
that *be of faith* are blessed with faithful Abraham." The
faith of Abraham was manifested throughout his life in
the doing of the things commanded by God. His course
of life was governed by the Word of God, and not by the
rules that ordinarily govern human conduct when men
are left to themselves. God's Word, obeyed from the

heart, made him a stranger and a pilgrim on earth; but it gave him also the prospect of "a better country, that is an heavenly;" and of a city that hath foundations, whose Maker and Builder is God.

The Lord's words to the Pharisees, who claimed Abraham for their father, are very important. He said to them: "If ye were Abraham's children ye would *do the works of Abraham*" — that is to say, works of faith. (John. 8:39). If, therefore, we "be of faith," it will be manifested in a *life* of faith, that is to say, a life of obedience to the Word of God, a life governed and regulated in all things by the law of Christ, a life that is directly contrary to "the course of this world." We must indeed keep always in mind that it is only in the power of the Holy Spirit that such a life can be lived; but the Spirit is given for that very purpose to *them that believe;* and our part is to trust, submit, and obey.

Not only was Abraham's faith counted to him for righteousness, but in addition a wonderful promise was given to him, for "the Scripture foreseeing that God would justify the heathen through faith, preached before the gospel unto Abraham, saying: In thee shall all nations be blessed" (v. 8). This is a remarkable passage. It reveals to us the broad scope of God's purpose in the call of Abraham. It shows that the promise of "blessing" to all nations meant the justifying of the heathen through faith. But most remarkable of all is that it speaks of the *before-preaching* of the gospel, that is, the preaching of the gospel long before the coming of the dispensation to which the gospel belongs. From this we may gather that the Greek verb *evangelloo,* which is rendered in our ver-

sion "preach the gospel," signifies God's message of salva
tion for *all the nations;* and we may properly give it that
meaning.

And what was the particular "blessing" which God purposed to bestow upon the nations of the world? Its
character is not described in Genesis, where the promise
is recorded; but here we are informed that "the blessing
of Abraham" was nothing less than "the promise of the
Spirit" (v. 14). This verse (Gal. 3:14) closes the subject begun at verse 2 — receiving the Spirit — it being
stated at the beginning of the passage that the Spirit is
received "through faith."

It is to be noted that neither Abraham, nor Isaac, nor
Jacob, nor their descendents for upwards of four hundred years were "under law." The promise, therefore,
was in no way related to the law, nor was its fulfilment
in anywise dependent upon the doing of the works of the
law. In fact it is expressly stated concerning the covenant God made with Abraham, that the law, which was
four hundred and thirty years after, could not disannul it,
that it should make the promise of none effect (v. 17).
Thus we learn that God's purpose in the call of Abraham
was not to be accomplished through the efforts of men in
doing the works of the law; and well may we be thankful
from the depths of our heart, that such was not to be
the method of its accomplishment. For the effect of the
law was, not the bringing down of *blessing* from heaven
upon the nations of the world, but the bringing of a *curse*
upon all who were and are "of the works of the law."
For it is written "Cursed is every one that continueth not
in all things that are written in the book of the law to do

them" (v. 10). Moreover, the Old Testament bore clear witness that no man is justified by the law in the sight of God, for it was written "The just shall live *by faith*" (v. 11). The expression "are of the works of the law" should be carefully noted. It is plainly a contrast to the expression "they which are of faith," and signifies the condition of those who are not living by faith, not counting upon God to work in them that which is well pleasing in His sight, but counting upon their own efforts and religious doings (of whatever sort they may be) to accomplish what can be accomplished only by the power of the Spirit of God.

Here then was the situation at the Lord's coming. God had promised "blessing" to all the nations of the world, but the law of God pronounced a "curse" Both the *law* and also *the promise* must be fulfilled. Could it be done? Yes. And it *has been done*. For—

"Christ hath redeemed us from the curse of the law, BEING MADE A CURSE FOR US (for it is written, cursed is every one that hangeth on a tree) ; that the *blessing of Abraham* might come to the Gentiles *through Jesus Christ,* that we might receive the promise of the Spirit by faith" (vv. 13, 14).

The great object therefore was that we should "receive the promise of the Spirit," that being "the blessing" God had promised through Abraham and his Seed (Christ). When the time came for the fulfilment of that promise, God sent forth His Son to do and to suffer what must needs be done and suffered, and what He alone could do and suffer, in order that the great promise of the Spirit

might be received by simple "faith." That work was the
enduring by Him of the judgment justly due us for our
sins. That judgment is here described by the short but
expressive word "curse;" and this calls our attention to a
divinely marvellous equation found in verses 10 and 13
in each of which the words "curse" and "cursed" occur,
and in each of which the statements made are given a
firm support by the conclusive words "it is written." It
will be seen by an examination of those verses that there
has been a perfect balancing of the heavy account that
was against us, whereby the inflexible justice of God has
been fully vindicated and satisfied.

First we have God's testimony as to the condition of
the *very best part* of the human race, those who were
commendably striving to justify themselves by their efforts at doing "the works of the law." All such were
"under the curse: for it is written, Cursed is every one
that continueth not in all things which are written in the
book of the law to do them." The curse, therefore, was
due and it *must be borne.* But Christ takes the place of
those who deserved it. "Christ hath redeemed us from *the
curse of the law,* being made a curse for us: for it is written, *cursed* is every one that hangeth on a tree."

To "redeem," in the sense of the word here used, is
to pay the full amount due for the ransom of a forfeited
property. Therefore it was necessary, not only that
Christ should die, and should die by violence — shedding
His blood to atone for the sins of His people — but that
He should die *on the tree,* in order that His people might
be redeemed from "the *curse* of the law." The aspect of
redemption emphasized in Galatians is that connected with

the *cross,* rather than that connected with the *blood,* the latter being not mentioned in Galatians. For the thing upon which stress is laid in Galatians is — not the forgiveness of our sins, for which the price paid was the precious blood of Christ—but our being separated, completely cut off as Christ was by the infamy of the cross, from "this present evil world," and particularly from its religious systems and doings. The question of the forgiveness of our sins, and of our peace with God, does not come into view at all in Galatians as it does in Ephesians 1:7, Colossians 1:14 and 20, and many other Scriptures where the *blood* of Christ is referred to. In Galatians it is altogether a question of our walk *in* the world as those who have been crucified *to* the world. Paul tells us of his own position with reference to the world, saying: "I have been crucified with Christ;" and he comes back to this again at the close of the Epistle in the strong words: "But God forbid that I should glory, save in the cross of our Lord Jesus Christ, by Whom (or *whereby,* marg.) the world is crucified unto me, and I unto the world" (6:14).

The truth of the gospel so forcibly declared in these words is that the believer in Christ is identified with Him in the shame and reproach of the cross, so as to be, with respect to the world, like one crucified, or in other words an object of the extremest aversion and contempt. This is "the offence of the cross" (Gal. 5:11). How does "the world" regard one who hangs on the gallows? Let it regard us as such. But we must not lose sight of the other side of it, namely, that we are to regard the world as "crucified to us," that is to say as a thing to be shunned and despised.

Thus, by the Lord's death on the cross, the curse is removed from us who trust in Him; and moreover the way is prepared for God to bestow "the promise of the Spirit" on all who believe.

We feel that enough is not made of the fact that the giving of the Spirit was a "promise" of God, and a promise of such vast importance that an entire dispensation, during which God's dealings in grace extend to all the nations of the world, has been given to it; and that furthermore, for its fulfilment, the Son of God must come as Man and *die on the cross.* As we meditate upon the greatness of this "promise," we shall see more fulness of meaning than otherwise we might in the Lord's words to His disciples: "And behold, I send *the promise of My Father upon you*" (Luke 24:49). Two things in this saying of the Lord should be noticed; first, that "the promise" was that of the *Father,* indicating that those who should receive the Spirit were to be His children; and second, that it was *Christ* Who was to send the Spirit to them.

It is easy to see that the Lord was here repeating what John the Baptist had preached at the beginning, namely "He shall baptize you with the Holy Ghost," which shows that John was the herald of this present dispensation of the Holy Spirit.

The apostle Peter, on the day of Pentecost, used words corresponding exactly with those of the Lord, saying of Christ: "Therefore being by the right hand of God exalted, and having received *of the Father* the *promise of the Holy Ghost,* HE hath shed forth *this"* (Acts. **2:33**). And again he spoke of the Spirit as "the promise" saying: "And ye shall receive the gift of the Holy Ghost; for *the promise* is unto you, and to your children, and to all that are afar off (Gentiles), even as many as the Lord our God shall call."

In Ephesians Paul also uses the expression the "Holy Spirit of promise," showing that the coming of the Holy Spirit as the gift of God unto those of all nations whom He should call in His grace, was the subject of Old Testament promise and prophecy. Thus the apostle Peter could say that *"all* the prophets from Samuel and those that follow after, as many as have spoken, have likewise foretold of these days" (Acts. **3:24**).

We conclude then that the Holy Spirit is given to them that believe, in order that God's purposes might be fulfilled in them through the power of the Spirit; and that the work which must needs have been done in order that the Spirit might be given, was fully accomplished by the Lord Jesus Christ in dying *on the cross.*

VIII.

WHEREFORE THEN THE LAW?
(Gal. 3:19).

Since it was not possible that any law could be given that could have given life to dying men, and not possible that righteousness should come by the law, the question asked in verse 19 of chapter 3 naturally arises, "Wherefore then the law?" Why was there, between the giving of the promise to Abraham, and its fulfilment through Christ, that long and seemingly fruitless period of the law? What purpose did it serve? This is indeed a deeply interesting question; and to it the Epistle to the Galatians supplies an answer which, while not complete, is sufficient, and is pertinent to the special subject of this Epistle. The answer, given in few words, is: "It was added for the sake of transgressions, until the Seed should have come to Whom *the promise* was made, having been ordained through angels in the hand of a mediator. Now a mediator is not of one; but God is one" (3:19, 20 Gr.). This passage is not so clear as to be apprehended without effort; but it is well worth inquiring into. The statement that the law was "added" is significant. This indicates that the law was not a part of the scheme of redemption, directly contributing thereto, but was "added to" or superimposed upon that plan. To the same effect it is said in Romans 5:20, "Moreover the law *entered*," literally *came in by the way,* as we would say of a thing not bearing directly upon, or contributing directly to the accomplishment of the matter in hand.

And here we would submit to the judgment of our readers a proposition which we deem to be important. This dispensation of the Holy Spirit is sometimes spoken of as a "parenthesis," that is to say, a matter not related directly to the main subject but which interrupts the course of the theme, and could be dropped out without being missed. According to that idea, God's dealings with the nation Israel and His purpose for them are regarded as the essential features of His great plan for the ages, the era of the church being viewed as a "parenthesis," because it supposedly breaks in upon God's dealings with Israel, which are to be resumed at the close of this dispensation.

But we maintain on the contrary that according to what is clearly stated in Galatians the *main line* of God's dealings is that of His covenant with Abraham and his Seed, leading into blessing to all the nations. In other words, God's main line of working is not "under the law" but "under the promise." For Abraham was never under the law. The *law* then and not the church-age was the "parenthesis," for it interrupted, during a period of about fifteen hundred years, God's dealings in the line of the promise, just as the Hagar episode was a "parenthesis" in Abraham's personal history, interrupting for a time his relations with the true wife, Sarah.

Moreover, the beginning and the ending of the parenthetical era of the law are *definitely marked*. The law was "four hundred and thirty years after" the promise (v. 17); and its duration was only "until the Seed should come to Whom the promise was made" (v. 19). Indeed the whole point of the argument here is that the law, being a parenthesis interposed between "the promise" and the "Seed" by Whom it was to be fulfilled, cannot be taken as disannulling or as modifying in anywise the terms of the promise. "The covenant that was confirmed before of God *to* (not *in*) Christ, the law, which was four hundred and thirty years after, *cannot disannul*" (v. 17). On the other hand, the law could not, and did not, promote in anywise the fulfilment of the promise. "For if the inheritance be of the law" — that is, be attained through the instrumentality of the law —" it is no more of promise: but God gave it (the inheritance) to Abraham *by promise*" (v. 19). Hence the law had nothing to do with the accomplishment of the purpose in view in the giving of the promise.

It is, we think, highly important to grasp the fact that this present era of the Holy Spirit, so far from being a "parenthesis," interrupting the progress of God's main plan of operations, is in fact the very era that was in contemplation when God called Abraham and gave him the promises; and to grasp also the related fact that the law was truly a parenthetical period, during which the execution of "the promise" was necessarily suspended.

The verse last quoted brings to view another characteristic word of the Epistle, namely "the inheritance"; and we would take special notice of this word because the thought it conveys is intimately connected with what we regard as the main subject of the Epistle — "Our liberty in Christ."

WHEREFORE THEN THE LAW? 89

But before considering the subject of the inheritance, we have to inquire into the reason for the bringing in of the long period of the law, occupying about fifteen hundred years, thus greatly delaying the fulfilment of the promise, while not apparently contributing anything to its accomplishment. We may indeed be quite sure the era of the law was needed, and that it did not last a moment too long. For we have the explicit statement that "when the fulness of the time was come" *then* "God sent forth His Son" (4:4) ; and of course, He could not have come any sooner. Hence the law filled up an interval of time which had to elapse in any case.

Another statement concerning the law is made in this connection, namely, that it *could not be the agency where by the promise was to be fulfilled and the inheritance gained.* The reason is that, if the inheritance be gained by means of the law, it would no longer be *by promise,* and since God made it at the beginning a matter of *pro mise,* He could not change the character of His dealings and make it a thing to be gained through the law. An unconditional promise rests for its fulfilment *solely upon the good faith of the one who makes it.*

The bearing of this part of the argument will be evident if we keep in mind that the false teachers to whom the Galatians were listening were endeavouring to change the accomplishment of God's purposes in His people from the basis of *grace* ("the promise") on which it rests secure, to the basis of *human works* ("the law"). So Paul strenuously insists that the bringing in of the period of law, which was only a parenthesis, did not and could not change either the basis on which God had caused His pur-

pose to rest or the method of its accomplishment. **God**
gave the inheritance to Abraham *by promise;* hence God
must fulfil it *apart from all works of law,* and regardless
of man's failure when tested by law.   And just here we
may anticipate our remarks concerning "the inheritance"
to the extent of pointing out that the receiving of the
Spirit is *included in the inheritance,* since the Spirit is
"the Earnest of our inheritance until the redemption of
the purchased possession" (Eph. 1:13, 14).   We see
then that *all* the inheritance of the sons of God *must come
to them by grace alone,* that is, as the *gift* of God, apart
from all works of their own.

We are now prepared for consideration of those rather
obscure words: "It (the law) was ordained by angels in
the hand of a mediator.   Now a mediator is not of one,
but God is One."
What comes into view here is the great difference between the two covenants, a difference illustrated by the
remarkable allegory in chapter 4, to which allusion has
already been made.   The point of difference indicated in
the words last quoted is that the covenant of grace (the
promise) has *but one party to it*—God Himself; whereas
the law was a *two-part* covenant; for it was ordained by
the agency of angels in the hand of a mediator.   Now a
mediator is not (and cannot be) the mediator of *one*
party.   There must be *two parties* to a covenant (or agreement) made through the offices of a mediator.   But God
Who made the promise is *One.*
The covenant of the law "from Mount Sinai" (4:25)
was ratified between God and the children of Israel, that
is, "Israel after the flesh" (1 Cor. 10:18).   Hence it re-

quired for its fulfilment the full performance *by both parties* of all their respective undertakings. But Israel broke that covenant less than forty days after it had been ratified (Ex. 32). Thereupon, His covenant being broken (according to the words, "Which My covenant they brake, saith the Lord"—Jer. 31:32), God, as the result of Moses' intercession, took them up again on a different basis, saying: "I will proclaim the Name of the Lord before thee, and *will be gracious to whom I will be gracious, and will show mercy on whom I will show mercy*" (Ex. 34:19). It was purely a matter of *grace* and in fulfilment of His promise to the fathers that God brought the people of Israel into Canaan. As stated by Jeremiah: "The people which were left of the sword *found grace* in the wilderness" (Jer. 31:2). God was not bound by the covenant of Sinai any longer; though He continued His relations with Israel under the form of it.

But now, in view of what has been shown as to the impossibility of the covenant of law either changing or aiding the fulfilment of the promise, another question arises: "Is the law then *against* the promises of God?" It might seem so. But such is not the case. God Who made the promise Himself also gave the law. Hence the law could not be against the promise. In fact, the law might even have aided the promise *if it could have given life.* But, because of the infirmity of the flesh and the corruption of the heart of man, that which was "ordained to life" was "found to be unto death" (Rom. 7:10.) Hence Moses' ministry of the old covenant became "the ministration of *death*" and "the ministration of *condemnation*" (2 Cor. 3:7, 9).

Thus the law served to make evident the true state of
the natural man.   It brought to light the fact of the utter
ruin of the human race, proving that "the mind of the
flesh is enmity against God, for it is not subject to the
law of God, neither indeed can be" (Rom. 8:7. R. V.)
Needless to say, God could do nothing with a race of
beings that was not subject and could not be made subject,
to His authority.   The brief statement concerning the law
that "it was added because of transgressions" can be
understood in the light of other Scriptures as signifying
God's plan, through the trial of a selected nation by means
of the law, *to prove the necessity for blood-redemption
and a new birth,* in other words the necessity for salvation by grace through the redemption that is in Christ
Jesus.   Thus we read in Romans 5:20, that "the law
entered that the offence might abound"; and in Romans
7:7, 13, that the knowledge of sin came by the law, and
that thereby sin became exceeding sinful.

It is clear, therefore, that the law did not change the
condition of those who were directly under law, and was
not intended to do so.   It served rather to bring out
and make evident the enmity and rebellion of the natural
heart of man, thus showing the necessity of a *change of
heart,* which is the work of this present age of grace.

This is the significance of verse 22 of our chapter
(Galatians 3): "But the Scripture hath concluded (lit.
shut up) all things under sin that the promise (that is
the Holy Spirit) might be given to them that believe."
In what sense are we to understand that the Scripture—
the written law of God—has shut up all things (the "all"
is neuter gender requiring the substantive "things") under
sin?   This must be understood in the sense that in the

light of man's trial under the law, it is seen that the whole creation (man's inheritance) is under the dominion of sin, and that there is need of *redemption,* not only of the persons of those whom God purposes to save, but of the "inheritance" as well.

Furthermore, the object of the law is declared to be "that every mouth may be stopped, and *all the world* may become guilty before God" (Rom. 3:19). This was manifestly a necessary preliminary to the dispensation of grace. For since God purposed to save men solely by grace, through faith, it was needful to show that all men, even the very best of them, were alike "guilty" and were equally dependent upon the undeserved mercy of God. Pardon is *not for the innocent,* but for the guilty; hence a man must be convicted of sin before he will seek pardon or is eligible for it. God therefore gives to all men the opportunity *now* to own themselves "guilty" and to accept pardon as God's gracious gift through Jesus Christ, and on the righteous ground that He, the Just One, suffered for the sins of those who accept God's Mercy offered by the gospel.

But there was another distinct purpose of the law, namely, it served to guard or keep the nation of Israel as a separate people up to the time of the coming of Christ and His presentation of Himself to that people. For we must not suppose that the Word of God given to the Israelites was "of none effect" (see Rom. 9:6), even though the nation as a whole transgressed it. There was always, even when things were at their worst in Israel, a believing remnant (seven thousand even in the days of Ahab). Not that these kept the whole law or were saved by it; but they were "Israelites indeed," because

they had "the circumcision of the heart," and they were
saved through faith. Paul has in mind this believing
remnant whose hearts were perfect toward God, and
who were always the real "Israel" (Rom. 9:6), known
of God though unrecognized by the eye of man. For let
us clearly understand that faith is always and altogether
a matter of *the heart.* It is an attitude of the heart toward God, manifesting itself in a voluntary submission to
His Word.

Paul speaks of those believing Israelites as minor children (and includes himself among them), saying: "We
were kept (*i. e.* guarded) under the law, shut up unto
the faith which should afterwards be revealed. Wherefore the law was our schoolmaster to bring us unto
Christ, that we might be justified by faith. But after
faith is come we are no longer under a schoolmaster"
(v. 23-25). The word "pedagogue" (translated "schoolmaster") is compounded of two words meaning *a child*
and *to bring* (or lead), the duty of the pedagogue being
to take charge of the young children and bring them to
school. Thus the pedagogue was responsible for the care
of the children. But on the other hand the children were,
in a sense, in bondage to the pedagogue. Thus Paul
illustrates the law in its guardianship of the true-hearted
Israelites. "The heir," he says, "as long as he is a child*
differeth nothing from a servant, though he be lord of all;
but is under tutors and governors until the time appointed of the father. Even so, we, when we were children (minors) were *in bondage* under the elements of the
world" (4:1-3).

Thus the law served a special purpose of guardianship

---

*This is not the ordinary word for "child," nor that for "son," nor
that for "babe," but a special word meaning a *minor* or one under age.

over those who, like the writer of Psalm 119, loved the law of God, rejoiced in His statutes and judgments, and delighted greatly in His commandments. But that guardianship was only "unto Christ"; for, says Paul, "after that *faith is come* we are no longer under a pedagogue."

Let us notice that "the faith" is what succeeded and displaced "the law" as a dispensation; and that the *coming of Christ* is the coming of "the faith." Before Christ came, faith looked forward to Him. But now "faith" means nothing other and nothing less than trusting, submitting to, and obeying *from the heart,* Jesus Christ Who was crucified and Who rose from the dead. Faith, in the Bible-sense of the word, *does not exist apart from Jesus Christ;* and the value of faith lies not at all in the one who exercises it, but wholly and solely in the One believed in. Faith saves wholly and solely because of the merits of the One Whom God has given us to believe in, and because of the value and sufficiency in God's eyes of the work accomplished by Him. "*The* faith" has come; because the Christ of God has come, and has fulfilled all that was written of Him. Hence the dispensation of law has given way to that of grace; and under grace those who are of the faith of Jesus Christ are received into the family of God as sons. "For ye are all the children (or sons) of God by faith in Christ Jesus. For as many of you as have been baptized into (unto) Christ have put on Christ" (3:26, 27).

Baptism is here presented as figuratively accomplishing that which it represents—the putting off of the old man (having died to his authority) and the putting on the New Man, Christ Jesus. The death of the believer in association with Christ crucified is the door of escape from the old "bondage" of sin; and his association with Christ in resurrection is his entrance into "the liberty wherewith Christ hath made us free." Baptism is both the symbol and the witness on our part of the truth of what has taken place in our spiritual being through faith in Christ Jesus.

In Christ all national distinctions and the like disappear, and the fact that there is but "one baptism," for disciples out of all the nations whether men or women (Mat. 28:19, 20; Eph. 4:5), is a witness to the truth that all are "one in Christ Jesus." "There (*i. e.* in Chirst) is neither Jew nor Greek; there is neither bond nor free; there is neither male nor female; for ye are *all one in Christ*" (Gal 3:28).

Another consequence of being saved by grace through faith in Christ is stated in the next verse: "And if ye be Christ's, then are ye Abraham's seed and *heirs* according to the promise" (29).

We have then these two great things which the grace of God brings to us, namely, present "liberty," and a future "inheritance" Those things naturally attach to *sonship*. Being *sons* (as distinguished from bond-servants), we have liberty, and we have also the sure prospect of an inheritance. For "if children then *heirs;* heirs of God and *joint-heirs with Christ*" (Rom. 8:17). To the same effect we have in Gal. 4:7, the statement: "Wherefore thou art no more a bond-servant but a son; and if a son, then an *heir* of God through Christ."

Thus we can see something at least of the purpose served by the law, coming in as a parenthesis between the giving of the promise to Abraham and its fulfilment through Abraham's promised Seed, Jesus Christ. Further light on this subject is to be had through the allegory of the two covenants, considered later.

IX.

THE ADOPTION AND THE SPIRIT OF ADOPTION

One of the declared purposes for which God sent forth His Son, made of woman, made under the law, was "that we might receive the adoption."*

It is unfortunate that the English word "adoption" has in our modern usage a very different meaning to that of the Greek word used in Galatians 4:5, and in other Epistles of Paul. The "adoption" of a child into a family where he does not belong by birth is a very different thing from that "adoption" which we receive as a result of the redemption accomplished by our Lord Jesus Christ. The word means the *placing of a son,* and it points to the purpose of God to bring His children into "the inheritance" whereof they are made, by grace, the joint-heirs with Jesus Christ, "Whom He hath appointed *Heir of all things*" (Heb. 1:2).

The word "adoption" occurs only five times, all in the writings of Paul. A brief reference to each occurrence will suffice for a clear understanding of the meaning of the word, which is of much importance.

In Ephesians 1:5 it is recorded of us whom God has blessed with all spiritual blessings in Christ, and whom He had chosen in Him before the foundation of the world, that He had "predestinated us *unto the adoption* (of children) by Jesus Christ unto Himself." This does

---

*There is but one word in the original represented by the three words "adoption of sons.

not tell us what the adoption is, but tells us that God had
it in view from before the foundation of the world, and
that it was to be accomplished by Christ Jesus. The context also connects the adoption with our "inheritance"
(v. 11), and with the gift of the "Holy Spirit of Promise,
Who is the *Earnest* of our inheritance" (v. 13, 14).

In Romans 9:4, 5, is a list of the wonderful things
which pertained to *Israel,* which list is headed by "the
adoption." Hence, as *Gentiles,* we should have no part
in these things were it not that "the Israel of God" includes believing Gentiles, as well as believing Jews, the
former being just as truly the seed of Abraham as the
latter.

In Romans 8 we find the other two occurrences of the
word "adoption" and from these its meaning is clear.
The prominent subject of this great passage is the Spirit
of God (given to and dwelling in the children of God),
and the several ministries of the Spirit on their behalf. We
find in this Scripture the same characteristic words as in
Galatians—children, bondage, liberty, the inheritance, the
heirs, the flesh, the Spirit, the adoption. Verse 15 reads·
"For ye have not received the (a) spirit of *bondage*
again to fear, but the Spirit of adoption, whereby we
cry, 'Abba, Father.'"

This verse speaks plainly (as does Galatians 4:5) of
the work of the Spirit in making real to the children of
God His relation to them of "Father," so that they can
intelligently and confidently address Him as "Father."
But here the Holy Spirit is called "the Spirit of *Adoption.*" As such He enables us to anticipate, and look
forward to, and patiently wait for, *the adoption itself,*
mentioned in verse 23, which tells us that we are "wait-

ing for the adoption, to wit, the redemption of our body."
The adoption then is still *future*. It is that which we
"hope for," the "glory" into which the children of God
are to be brought in association with Christ at His coming
again. It includes the taking possession of the redeemed
creation, which shall then be "delivered from the bondage
of corruption into the liberty of the glory of the children
of God" (Rom. 8:21). It is what is referred to in the
corresponding passage in Ephesians (1:13) as "the redemption of the purchased possession to the praise of His
glory."

All these Scriptures present the Spirit of God as the
present possession of God's children, as the "Earnest" or
"First fruits" of the eternal inheritance which they are
to share with Christ as His co-heirs; and they all speak
of the Father sparing not His own Son, but sending Him
forth to redeem those for whom the adoption is prepared,
thus making way for the coming of the Holy Spirit into
their hearts.

The adoption is therefore a comprehensive term embracing all those glorious things which eye hath not seen,
nor ear heard, and which have not entered into the heart
of man—"the things which God hath prepared for them
that love Him." And it is only through the Spirit and
by faith that these things can be known, for "God hath
revealed them unto us *by His Spirit;* for the Spirit
searcheth all things, yea, the deep things of God." For
"we have received not the spirit of the world, but the
Spirit which is of God; that we *might know the things
that are freely given to us of God"* (1 Cor. 2:9-12).

When a child is born heir to vast possessions and prop-
erties his human spirit—"the spirit *of man* that is in

him"—enables him to know those things, to appreciate to some extent their value, and to enjoy their prospective possession; for they are "the things of a man." But "the things of God knoweth no man; but the Spirit of God." In proportion, therefore, as we are filled with the Spirit, and yielded to the Spirit for the purpose of a heart-interest in the things of our Lord Jesus Christ, to that extent will the Spirit take of that which is Christ's and show it unto us; and to a corresponding extent will we be set free from interest in and affection for the things that are seen—the things human and temporal.

The foregoing Scriptures reveal further that the inheritance promised to Abraham was far greater, more vast and more glorious, than appears by the Old Testament records. To the same effect are the words of Romans 4: 13, "For the promise that he should be the *heir of the world,* was not to Abraham or to his seed through the law, but through the righteousness of faith." There is nothing in Genesis to show that God promised to Abraham that he should be the heir *of the world,* but to us has been given by the New Testament Scriptures certain information of great value which in other ages was not made known to the children of men. God communi cated to Moses and inspired him to write only so much of what He had promised to Abraham, His "friend," as He was pleased to make known to "Israel after the flesh." Hence the record of His promise of possessions in the world extended no further than the land bounded by the Mediterranean Sea on the West and the Euphrates River on the East; for the promise to the *earthly* people is confined to that. But God had in view also a *heavenly* people, for whom He had in store things of surpassing value and glory; and it is evident that He spake to Abraham of those things also. For it is written of Abraham and others of the household of faith that they saw the promises afar off, and were persuaded of them, to such an extent that they showed by their lives that they were seeking "a better country, that is, an *heavenly;* wherefore God is not ashamed to be called their God; for He hath *prepared for them a city."* (Heb. 11:13-16).

Evidently that city—the heavenly Jerusalem, which in Galatians 4:26 is spoken of as "the mother of us all"—was a very bright prospect in Abraham's outlook. It was because he was looking for the city which hath the foundations, whose Architect and Builder is God, that Abraham shunned the cities of earth, "dwelling in tents with Isaac and Jacob, the heirs with him of the *same promise"* (Heb. 11:9, 10). The promise of the heavenly Jerusalem, the eternal home of God and His redeemed people, is the greatest of all promises. There can be nothing higher, greater or more glorious than that, whether for the saints of this dispensation or those of any other. It is a great mistake, therefore, to assign to Abraham (as some of our modern expositors do) a position of inferiority in the glory to that of the saved of this present age.

It is a mistake also to exclude the earth from the inheritance of the saints. Heaven and earth will not be separated then as now; for the New Jerusalem will come down out of heaven from God; and the kings of the earth will bring their honour and glory into it. (Rev. 21:2, 24).

In the passage in Ephesians which speaks of our inheritance in Christ, and of the Holy Spirit being given
as the Earnest thereof until the redemption of the purchased possession, we read of the purpose of God which
He hath purposed in Himself, "that in the dispensation
of the fulness of times He might gather together *in one*
all things in Christ, both which are *in heaven and which
are on earth*" (Eph. 1:9-14).   Heaven and earth will
then be "one."

The "purchased possession" of Ephesians 1:14, is
plainly the ransomed creation now groaning under the
bondage of corruption (Rom. 8:19-21).   It is "the field"
of the parable, to purchase which the Man (Christ)
"went and sold all that He had" (Mat. 13:44).

In the Epistle to the Hebrews, wherein the Lord Jesus
Christ is set forth as "the Heir of all things," it is "the
world to come" (lit. *the habitable earth to come*) which
is presented as the most prominent feature of the inheritance of Christ and of "the heirs of salvation"
(Heb. 1:2, 14; 2:5-10).   Furthermore, it is declared
in the same passage that, for the purpose of possessing
and governing the earth, God laid not hold of angels, but
lad hold of the *seed of Abraham* (Heb. 2:10, marg.).
And these seed of Abraham are declared to be, as in
Galatians, *the children of God.*   Finally, this prospective
inheritance of the earth on the part of those who are
"joint-heirs with Christ," is spoken of as "the *heavenly*
calling" (Heb. 3:1).

There is regrettable confusion on this subject in pre-
sent-day teaching.   Thus, in a current magazine we read
under the title "The Inheritance" a comment on the

words of Psalm 37:11, "But the meek shall inherit the earth," as follows:

> "Christians often claim this as a promise that they will inherit the earth. But the inheritance of the true church is not the earth, but it is the heavenly place, as the greatest Epistle of the New Testament, Ephesians, tells us."

Whether Ephesians be the greatest Epistle of the New Testament we have no means of knowing; but certainly it does *not* tell us that the "inheritance" of the saints is not the earth. Continuing our quotation·

> "But who are the meek to inherit the earth? The Jewish people who will turn to the Lord in the days of the coming trouble * * With this agrees perfectly the one beatitude of our Lord in the Sermon on the Mount, "Blessed are the meek, for they shall inherit the earth.' The meek are the godly Israelites of the last days."

It is deplorable that statements of a radical sort like the foregoing should be recklessly made to the Lord's people, without even the shadow of an attempt to sup port them by evidence from the Word of God—statements which are directly contrary to the clearest testimony of Scripture. For it is most plain from the passages we have just cited, and from others, that the Lord Jesus Christ as Son of Man, is the *Heir of the earth* and all the creatures therein (see particularly Psalm 8, and Heb 2:5-8); and that the church will share the inheritance with Him. It is also plain that the earthly people

Israel in the coming day of their national restoration will not inherit the earth, but will occupy only a small part thereof.

The earth in the coming age, when all the effects of the curse shall have been removed, will be glorious and beautiful beyond our powers to imagine. Moreover, it will *be filled with the glory of the Lord* as the waters cover the sea (Isa. 11:9; Heb. 2:14). Let us therefore hold fast the prospect of inheriting the earth, which our Lord has redeemed, and on which the precious blood of redemption was shed.

The Spirit is given to the children of God for the purpose, amongst others, of taking of that which is Christ's (the ransomed creation being among "the things of Christ") and showing it unto us (John 16:13-15). Hence we should be delivered wholly, as to our affections and desires, from "this present evil world" (Gal. 1:4), seeing that, on the one hand the cross of Christ separates us from it, and on the other hand the Spirit of Adoption has been given as the Earnest of our Inheritance, and as the Revealer of its coming glories.

We have missed much of the truth of God if we have failed to see God's delight in His creation, and His purpose to ransom it from the bondage of corruption, to renew and glorify it, and to enter with His redeemed people into the possession and enjoyment of it. In the eighth chapter of Proverbs is a glowing description of the Son of God, Who is there presented as the Wisdom of God (see also 1 Cor. 1:24), first creating and then "rejoicing in the habitable part of His earth" (v. 31). This rejoicing in the ransomed "Inheritance" is one of the things which He offers to share (and *will* share) with His beloved co-heirs.   But unhappily this blessed prospect is blotted out of the view of many of these by a teaching which declares the earth to be unspiritual, and beneath the regard of the children of God.   This false idea which sets forth that matter is unspiritual and evil, was (and is) one of the main tenets of gnosticism, which was the greatest opponent of Christianity in the first century.   It has been revived in our day in the teachings of Mrs. Eddy, by which thousands are deluded; and even prominent teachers among the Lord's true people are telling them that the inheritance of the earth is not among those "spiritual blessings" wherewith we are blessed in Christ Jesus (Eph. 1:3).   But this is a great mistake.   Christ has been made "Head over *all things* to the Church" (Eph. 1:22) which will share the "all things" (*both* which are in heaven and *which are on earth*) with Him.   Let us not seek to be more "spiritual" than the Wisdom of God.

X

UNTIL CHRIST BE FORMED IN YOU
Gal. 4 : 19.

It would be a grave error to suppose that God's purpose in calling out of the world a people for His Name is merely to save them from eternal judgment and to have them with Him in heaven. It would be equally an error to suppose that the purpose of the ministry of the gospel is merely to bring sinners to Christ that they might receive from Him the forgiveness of sins and the gift of eternal life. The reconciliation of the sinner and his regeneration, making him a child of God, is but *the beginning* of the work of the gospel and of the Holy Spirit in his heart. The regeneration of a repentant sinner is the work of but a moment. There remains, however, a work which, in the mind of Paul (who understood its importance) called for an intensity of effort, and awakened an intensity of anxiety, beyond anything displayed by him in preaching Christ to the unconverted.

The false teachers referred to in Galatians were not hindering the preaching of the gospel to the unsaved. They were hindering the work of the gospel and the ministry of the Spirit of God *in the hearts of God's children.* We can form an idea as to God's estimate of the value of that work from the earnestness of utterance which characterizes the Epistle as a whole, and particularly from the verse containing the words of our chapter-heading: "My little children, of whom I travail in birth again until *Christ be formed in you*" (4 : 19). The entire verse

is an impetuous outburst of feeling.   It interrupts with
startling abruptness the course of the exhortation the
apostle was giving, showing that he could not refrain
himself from the expression of what was in his heart,
even so long as was needed to finish the sentence. There
is, moreover, deep tenderness and affection in the words
"my little children." Then the acuteness of his solicitude
and his strivings for them are likened to travailing in
birth. And a protracted period of labour-pains it was,
since it was to continue until the desired work should be
accomplished in them. Finally the object of his striving
on their behalf is declared in the words "until Christ be
formed in you."

This then, is *the full object* that God has in view for
those whom He calls into His household—that Christ be
formed in them. And the means employed for that purpose are, the Holy Spirit working in the saint, in co-opera
tion with a faithful ministry of the Word.

Again we observe the close parallel between the teaching of Galatians and that of Romans (chapters 5 to 8
especially). For in Romans 8 the passage which treats
of the Spirit of God, the Adoption, and the Inheritance
(to which we have referred) is immediately followed by
a clear statement of the *purpose* of God for those whom
He has saved and made His children, and for whom such
a glorious inheritance has been prepared (verses 28-30).
Speaking of them as "the *called* according to *His purpose,*" the apostle says: "For whom He did foreknow, He
also did predestinate to be *conformed to the image of His
Son,* that He might be the Firstborn among many
brethren" (Rom. 8:29).

We have here the purpose of God for His children, namely, that they should be conformed in character or "image" to His Son; but in Galatians we have the Divine Agencies by which this great purpose of God is to be carried out—the Spirit striving against the flesh, and the ministry of the Word, which works effectually in them that believe.

From Ephesians 4:7-16 we learn that to the same end the gifts of ministry from the risen Lord have been bestowed, those gifts being "for the work of the ministry, for the edifying of the body of Christ; *till we all come* in the unity of the faith and of the knowledge of the Son of God unto a *perfect* (*i. e.* fully developed) *man,* unto the measure of the stature of the fulness of Christ."

It is well for each of us to have as clear an idea as possible of what God purposes to work in us, so that we may give our hearts to that purpose, seeking to be fellow-labourers with God in its accomplishment, and using whatever gifts He has bestowed upon us to that end.

The same matter is very strongly presented in Colossians, where Paul speaks of the ministry committed to him to make Christ known among the Gentiles, in which connection he says: "Whom we preach, warning every man, and teaching every man in all wisdom, that we may present every man *perfect in Christ Jesus*"—that is to say, fully conformed to His image, or (as in Galatians) "till Christ be formed" in each one. Then he adds this strong statement: "Whereunto I also labour, *striving* according to His working, which worketh in me *mightily*" (Col. 1:27-29).

From this we learn that Paul regarded his ministry as not merely making Christ known to sinners for their salvation, but more particularly as preaching Christ for the *perfecting of saints;* and that his ministry was not fulfilled even by preaching, warning and teaching, but required also *labouring,* and even *striving,* and that not in his own energy merely, but in the working of the Spirit of God, working in him "mightily."

Manifestly then, the perfecting of the saints is a matter of the greatest moment; and there is need to emphasize this because it is virtually lost sight of and ignored at the present time. God requires *full-grown men in Christ,* not only for service, testimony and fruit-bearing in this age, but also for important administrative duties in the age to come. It may be well to bring again to mind that the final aim of God's dealings with the people of His choice is that they may *bear fruit,* and that their fruit may abound. Since maturity, or full growth, is essential to fruit-growing, we clearly perceive why so much importance is attached to the perfecting of the saints. God's purpose in sowing the good seed is not attained in the blade, nor even in the ear, but in the *full corn in the ear* (Mark 4:28).

We should therefore give earnest heed to the warnings found in Galatians and Colossians concerning things that tend to defeat the working of God, in the carrying out of His plans for the perfecting of His saints. Those in Galatia were being put on the wrong track altogether; for notwithstanding that they had begun their life as children of God *"in the Spirit,"* they were now thinking to be *"made perfect in the flesh."* This is called by Paul *a turning back* to the weak and beggarly elements, and as manifesting a "desire again to be in bondage" (Gal. 4: 9). When they knew not God they did service (literally *were in bondage to*) them which by nature are no gods. But now, after coming to know God, or rather having become known of God (accepted and acknowledged as His), how surprising that they should turn back to the old observances! For as heathen worshippers of idols they had observed "days, and months, and times, and years." And now, notwithstanding their deliverance from that and every other form of "bondage" through the cross of Christ, they are returning to it again! This leads Paul to say: "I am afraid of you, lest I have bestowed upon you labour in vain" (v. 11).

Why should the apostle fear lest he might have bestowed upon those Galatian converts labour in vain? Was he doubtful of their salvation? Evidently not; for he had just said they were "all the children of God by faith in Jesus Christ," that they were *heirs* according to the promise, and that God had sent forth the Spirit of His Son into their hearts. He had even declared their present and eternal relations with God in the most emphatic language, saying: "Wherefore thou are no more a servant, but a son; and if a son then *an heir of God through Christ.*" That was all settled when they repented and believed in Jesus Christ.

No, it was not his labour in preaching to them as sinners the gospel of God concerning His Son, that Paul feared might prove fruitless. His anxiety was solely in regard to the labour he had expended in ministering Christ to them *for their spiritual growth.* The anxiety, the care, and the incessant labours of the husbandman begin *when the seed has sprouted into the tender plant,* and continue during all the period of growth. The toil and cost of plowing and planting might all be lost through *neglect in cultivation.* It is evident therefore that what filled the apostle's heart with anxiety, causing it indeed to overflow into a letter which (contrary to his usual custom) he wrote with his own hand (6:11), was the prospect that, through the meddlesomeness of zealous teach-- ers of law-works, all his own labours might be rendered fruitless. Thus our attention is called sharply to the fact that *God's work through the Holy Spirit is needed for growth in Christ*—leading on to the bearing of fruit for God—*just as much as for regeneration.* It is *only by the Spirit* that one of Adam's fallen race is re-born into the family of God, "the household of faith" (6:10). So too it is only *by the Spirit* that the child of God can be conformed to the image of Christ (2 Cor. 3:18), and can bear fruit, "the fruit of the Spirit" (5:22, 23), for the glory and acceptance of God.

Having all this in view, Paul now turns from *warning* and *rebuke* to earnest and tender *entreaty,* saying "Brethren, *I beseech you,* be as I am; for I am as ye are" (4:12). Paul was free in Christ from the bondage of religious ceremonial such as mentioned in verse 10— observing days, and months, and times, and years. He was separated by the cross of Christ from the world and all its barren doings whereby men in the corruption of the flesh, and having not the Spirit of God, seek to perfect themselves through religious rites and observances. He was living his life then in the flesh "by the faith of the Son of God." Hence he besought them to *be as he was*.

Moreover, he says for their encouragement, that he was as they were. We are apt to regard prophets, apostles and other holy men of old as if they were of a different order of beings—not common clay like ourselves. We need therefore to be told that "Elijah was a *man*, subject to like passions as we are" (Jam. 5:17), and that Paul was, in himself, just as weak as we ourselves. They were all but "earthen vessels" even as we. What was it then that made them different to other men? Simply and solely the grace of God given to all who believe. Thus in another place Paul testifies saying: "I am the least of the apostles, that am not meet to be called as apostle * *but *by the grace of God* I am what I am" (1 Cor. 15:9, 10). Yes, it was the grace of God toward that "chief of sinners" that made all the differ ence; and what we should by all means lay hold of is the fact that *God's grace is for us as much as for Him.*

What Paul specifically refers to in this connection is that he was like them in being *weak*. He reminds them of this, saying: "Ye know how through infirmity of the flesh (*bodily weakness*) I preached the gospel unto you at the first. And my temptation (the trial he had to bear) which was in my *flesh* ye despised not, nor rejected; but received me as an angel (messenger) of God, even as Christ Jesus" (See Mat. 10:40).

In other places the apostle mentions the "weakness" of his "bodily appearance," and his lack of gifts of oratory, explaining that his deficiencies in these endowments (which are regarded by many as special qualifications for

successful preaching and ministry) were in reality a
part of his equipment for the work to which God had
called him, the purpose being (to quote his own words)
"that the excellency of the power may be OF GOD, and not
OF US" (2 Cor. 4:7)—that is to say, that men might be
forced to admit that it was Divine power working
through this frail, defective instrument, and not the
mere power of nature; and that the glory of the results
accomplished through his ministry might be given to God,
the real Doer, and not to the instrument which He was
pleased to employ.   There is surely encouragement for
all who wish to serve the Lord Jesus Christ in the fact
that natural abilities, eloquence of speech, education,
learning, and other things greatly prized by "the flesh,"
are not essential, and may be even a hindrance rather than
a help, in that service.

Paul appeals also (verse 15) to their devotion and love
for himself at the first, bearing them witness that they
would have been willing even to have plucked out their
own eyes and given them to him.   "Where is then," he
sadly asks, "the blessedness ye spake of?"   His ministry
had brought them into the "blessedness" of knowing
their sins forgiven (Rom. 4:6-9) and their gratitude to
him at that time knew no bounds.   What had made the
difference?   Had *he* changed in any wise toward them?
"Am I therefore become your enemy, because I tell you
the truth?" (v. 16).   The truth is often resented if it
demands a change of our ways; but the faithful servant
of Christ will risk even the loss of friendship where the
truth is needed for correction of saints who have departed
from it.

Again, in verses 17 and 18, Paul refers to those teachers who were misleading the Galatians. We give a free rendering of those verses: "They are zealous after you, but not for your advantage. Yes, they would even exclude you from me, that ye might be zealous after them. But it is good to be zealous always in a good thing, and not only when I am present with you—" Here the apostle, overcome with tender concern for them and by his acute distress at the thought of his "little children" being thus beguiled away from him, breaks off the unfinished thought in order to declare his anxious care and the travail of his soul for them in the words upon which we have already commented.

And now he makes his final appeal, beginning with another question: "Tell me, ye that desire to be under the law, *do ye not hear the law?*" (v. 21). This leads to the allegory of the two covenants which we will discuss in the next chapter.

XI.

THE TWO COVENANTS
(Gal. 4:24).

We have here a fact of deepest interest, and one that never could have been known but by revelation, namely, that the incidents of Abraham's history resulting in the birth of Ishmael, who was born to Abraham by Hagar, and those resulting in the birth of Isaac, constituted an "allegory"; and that those incidents were brought to pass in order to illustrate the two great covenants—the covenant of Law, and the covenant of Grace.

Abraham is the man of God's purpose whom He had "called alone" (Isa. 51); and in this passage we have his two wives and his two sons, the wives representing the two covenants, which are likened to two mountains, and representing also the two cities—the earthly Jerusalem and the Jerusalem which is above. Thus we have five pairs of contrasted things, all connected with the one man of faith—two wives, two sons, two covenants, two mountains, two cities.

This allegory bears directly upon the main theme of Galatians—our *Liberty in Christ*—for it points out that the covenant which was ratified from Mount Sinai, represented by Hagar, genders to "bondage," in other words, brings forth children which are born into servitude, and hence are not *heirs;* whereas the covenant represented by Sarah brings forth to "liberty." Her children are all "free"; and they all have in prospect a glorious inheritance. It teaches moreover, that the children of the bond-

woman, *though her son was the first-born,* are to have no
share in the inheritance with the children of the free
woman: "For the son of the bond-woman *shall not be
heir* with the son of the free woman."

There is a vast amount of instruction (and that of the
deepest interest) in these five contrasted things, running
in two lines, both having their start in Abraham. Each
one of the things enumerated in one line has its answering feature in the other line; and yet there is a very great
difference between the two. The two wives represent,
respectively, the convenant of grace and the convenant
of law, and their two sons represent an earthly and a
heavenly people, a people in the one case born "after the
flesh," *i. e.* according to nature, and in the other a people
supernaturally born, "the children of promise," born "af
ter the Spirit." Moreover, we see here, as always, that
"that is not first which is spiritual, but that which is nat
ural, and afterwards that which is spiritual" (1 Cor. 15·
46).

Referring to the incidents of Abraham's family relations as recorded in Genesis 16, we learn that his marriage
with Hagar, and the birth of Ishmael which was the fruit
of it, was not an act of faith, but sprang from the im-
patience of nature—the flesh. It is written: "He that
believeth shall not make haste" (Isa. 28:16), that is,
shall not act in over-eagerness, but will quietly wait God's
time and His word as to any action to be taken. We do
not read that by faith Abraham, when he saw that Sarah
was barren and past childbearing because of age, took to
himself another wife. On the contrary, in so doing Abraham was not hearkening to the voice of God at all. Hence

it was not of faith. For "faith cometh by hearing, and hearing *by the Word of God.*" It was Sarah who suggested to Abraham that he should take Hagar to wife; "And Abraham hearkened to *the voice of his wife*" (Gen 16:2). In this he did as his father Adam had done (Gen. 3:17). God had given the promise that Abraham's seed which should come forth out of his own bowels should be like the stars of heaven for multitude, and it is recorded that "he believed in the Lord, and it was counted to him for righteousness" (Gen. 15:5, 6). How would God fulfil His promise? Abraham and Sarah did not wait until God should make known His way; but losing patience they acted, as we are all prone to do, in choosing a way of their own, and one that is according to nature, and looking to God to "bless the means." But God does not bless any but *His own appointed "means";* though He bears with marvellous patience our unbelieving ways, and doings.

We see then how possible, indeed how *easy* it is, for a man of faith to resort to the means employed by the flesh for the accomplishment of what God has promised to do, and which He will certainly bring to pass in His own time and way. The result of this act of Abraham was that a period of fourteen years passed ere God again visited him in grace.

There are several incidents on record in connection with Hagar and Ishmael which are of special interest in view of the typical significance given to them by the Holy Spirit in Galatians, who there makes Hagar the type of the earthly people, "Israel after the flesh." First we have Hagar's "affliction" before the birth of her son, answering to the affliction of Jacob's descendants in Egypt ere the nation Israel was born out of that land. Moreover the fact that Hagar was herself an Egyptian is not with out significance.

We have also the record that the angel of the Lord found her by a fountain of water in the wilderness (Gen. 16:7), recalling the words; "He found him (Israel) in the waste howling wilderness" (Deut. 32:10). Moreover, the angel of the Lord commanded Hagar to return to her place of servitude, but gave the promise; "I will multiply thy seed exceedingly, so that it shall not be numbered for multitude." Furthermore the angel said: "Behold, thou art with child and shalt bear a son, and shalt call his name Ishmael (*God shall hear*), because the Lord hath heard thy affliction." This part of the type was fulfilled in the history of the children of Israel when the Lord visited them in Egypt, saying: "I have surely seen *the affliction* of My people which are in Egypt, and have *heard their cry*" (Ex. 3:7).

The angel also said to Hagar: "And he (Ishmael) shall be a wild man; his hand will be against every man, and every man's hand against him; and he shall dwell in the presence of all his brethren" (Gen. 16:12). The word "wild" is literally "wild ass," an animal exceedingly hard to bring under control. God subsequently applies this word to Israel, calling the people "A wild ass used to the wilderness" (Jer. 2:24). The impossibility of keeping "Israel after the flesh" under the restraint of the law of God is what is suggested by this significant word. The statement, "his hand will be against every man, and every man's hand against him" is wonderfully prophetic of the perpetual enmity between the Israelite and the people of every other nationality, also of the fact that they were to come into contact with men of every nation. Nevertheless there is the forecast of comfort for the earthly people at their latter end in the promise "and he shall dwell in the presence of all his brethren." These words are recalled in Chapter 25 : 18, where it is recorded of Ishmael that "he died in the presence of all his brethren," showing that they were all gathered together.

It is also a point of interest, in view of the fact that Ishmael is expressly declared to be a type of the earthly Israel, that God, in answer to Abraham's plea for Ishmael, said : "As for Ishmael, I have heard thee : Behold, I have blessed him, and will make him fruitful, and will multiply him exceedingly : *twelve princes shall he beget,* and I will make him a great nation. But *My covenant* will I establish with *Isaac*" (Gen. 17 :20, 21).

Thus we are assured of God's continued interest in His earthly people, for whom there is a great future in the world. Doubtless there are other matters recorded of Ishmael for which corresponding incidents in Israel's history—past or future—might be found.

This mention of God's covenant sends us back to the seventeenth chapter of Genesis, which is notable for the frequent occurence in it of the word "covenant." God had made many promises to Abraham, but the word "covenant" is not found until we come to chapters 15 and 17, in which it occurs fourteen times. Thirteen of these are in chapter 17; and in three instances this covenant is called an "everlasting covenant" (verses 7, 13, 19). The Lord's words in this connection are:

"I will establish My covenant between Me and thee and thy seed after thee in their generations for an *everlasting covenant,* to be a God unto thee, and to thy seed after thee, and I will give thee the land of thy sojournings" (v. 7, 8, marg.).

And again, speaking of circumcision given as "a token of the covenant," God said:

"And My covenant shall be in your flesh for an *everlasting covenant"* (v. 13).

And finally:

"Sarah thy wife shall bear thee a son indeed; and thou shalt call his name Isaac; and I will establish My covenant with him for an *everlasting covenant,* and with his seed after him" (v. 19).

There are certain striking features about this particular covenant, to which heed should be given. First it is recorded that Abraham was at that time ninety-nine years old. This clearly identifies this promise as being the one to which reference is made in Romans 4: 17-22, where it is said that Abraham believed God "Who quickeneth the dead and calleth those things which be not" (Abraham's seed) "as though they were": that he "considered not his own body *now dead, when he was about an hundred years old,* neither yet the deadness of Sarah's womb; he staggered not at the promise of God through unbelief; but was made strong in *faith,* giving glory to God, and being fully persuaded that what He had promised He was able also to perform. And therefore it was imputed to him for righteousness." And we should not overlook the words that follow, nor fail to apply them to ourselves: "Now it was not written for his sake alone that it was imputed to him; but for *us also,* to whom it shall be imputed, if we believe on Him that raised up Jesus our Lord from the dead, who was delivered up for our offences, and raised again for our justification." This contemplates undoubtedly the *complete* justification of God's people by a life of faith.

Secondly: the covenant we are considering was accompanied by a change of Abraham's name as well as of that of Sarah. This was the mark of a new era in their existence, or rather of a *new existence.* Both were "as good as dead"; and moreover, their previous existence had been *barren* and *unfruitful.* They were now to begin a life of fruitfulness. But it is of the utmost importance to notice that this new and fruitful existence was brought about *wholly* by the intervention of God acting of His own will, and putting forth His own power to accomplish the desired result. Not until death had established its mastery over both Abraham and Sarah so far as concerns the possibility of having children, not until the resources of nature were exhausted, not until "the flesh" had reached the end of its activities, did God put forth His mighty power, showing Himself to be indeed the God who quickens the dead. In this lies a lesson of the greatest importance for spiritual children of Abraham.

Thirdly: this covenant was distinguished by the appointing of the rite of circumcision, the mark of death upon the flesh, as a "token" of the covenant. This is a further witness of the importance of nature to produce "fruit unto God," and of the fact that that which the flesh produces is "fruit unto death" (compare Rom. 7: 4, with 7: 5). Circumcision is a foreshadowing of the death of the Lord Jesus Christ on the cross, where He was "cut off" (Dan. 9:26); and this is the true circumcision of His people, as it is written: "In Whom also ye are circumcised with the circumcision made without hands in putting off the body of the flesh by the circumcision of Christ" (Col. 2:11, see Phil. 3:3). Since believers in Christ have the inward (which is the *true*) circumcision (Rom. 2:29), it is easy to understand the apostle's indignation with those who sought to impose upon them the outward circumcision, which was but a figure, now fulfilled and set aside.

It is significant that circumcision was appointed to Abraham as a token of that which had already taken place in his experience (death to the bringing forth of fruit); just as baptism is now the appointed figure of that which has taken place in the life of the believer, namely, death, burial and resurrection with Christ.

Thus God took up Abraham and Sarah when they had *come to the end of themselves,* so to speak, and placed them upon an entirely new basis, to walk before Him in newness of life, to bring forth fruit to His praise, and for a blessing to all the world. For the name of the promised son was to be "Isaac"—which means *laughter*—as Sarah said at his birth: "God hath made me to laugh, so that *all that hear* will laugh with me" (Gen. 21:6).

This then is the covenant which Paul, in Galatians, contrasts with the covenant that God made with the people of Israel at Mount Sinai. It is the covenant made with Abraham, not that made at Mount Sinai, which the apostle says is represented by Sarah, (the true wife who, however, was by nature barren) and which answers to the heavenly Jerusalem. The opening words of the account

given in Genesis 17 of this everlasting covenant should
be specially noted:

> "And when Abram was ninety years old and
> nine, the Lord appeared to Abram and said unto him,
> I am the *Almighty God*: walk before Me and be thou
> *perfect*" (Gen. 17:1).

God here reveals Himself for the first time by the
Name "God Almighty." This was in connection with
His promise to do that which was, according to nature,
an impossibility, and concerning which the question was
asked by Him: "Is anything too hard for the Lord?"
(Gen. 18:14). God recalled this in speaking to Moses,
saying "I AM the LORD, and I appeared unto Abraham
and unto Isaac and unto Jacob by the Name of *God Almighty,* but by My Name JEHOVAH was I not known
to them" (Ex. 6:2, 3). This Name—God Almighty—
is used but eight times in the books of Moses (seven
times in Genesis and once as above mentioned in Exo
dus). These are matched by eight occurences in the last
book of the Bible—Revelation. It is used in Job fre-
quently, but rarely elsewhere in the Old Testament. In
the New Testament its *only* occurence, apart from Revelation, is in the passage in which the Lord calls upon
His people to come out from every worldly association, to
be separate, and touch not the unclean thing; and in
which He gives the great promise: "And I will receive
you, and will be a Father unto you, and ye shall be My
sons and daughters, saith the *Lord Almighty*" (2 Cor. 6:
14-18).

God's call to Abraham at this time was to *walk* before
Him and be *perfect,* the latter being a word signifying

integrity or completeness. The correspondence with Galatians, where the "walk" of God's people and their being *perfected* are specially in view, is apparent.

But in the giving of this command, which was to change Abraham's life from barrenness to one of exceeding fruitfulness, God revealed Himself as *the Giver, through grace alone, of the supernatural power* whereby His purpose was to be carried out. Abraham's and Sarah's part in it was simply to *believe*. For it is written: "Through *faith* also Sara herself received strength to conceive seed, and was delivered of a child when she was past age, because she judged Him faithful who had promised. Therefore sprang there even of one, and him as good as dead, so many as the stars of the sky in multitude, and as the sand which is by the seashore innumerable" (Heb. 11:11, 12)

In the record given us in Genesis we find more of Sarah's incredulity than of her faith. But evidently her natural disposition to doubt, which is our's too, was in time overcome through the Word of God's grace, and she was at last enabled to "judge Him faithful Who had promised," even though the promise was the doing of a thing directly contrary to nature.

Particular attention should be given to the words "through faith Sara *received* strength," which show that the strength was God's, not Sarah's; for she only *received* it by faith, that is by counting upon God's faithfulness to *give* the power which she altogether lacked. It is so natural for us to look to ourselves instead of to God, that even in reading a passage like this we are apt to think that the result was due to the faith of Abraham and Sarah, instead of to the power and faithfulness of God.

Faith has no power whatever in itself. On the contrary it casts us wholly and in utter weakness upon the power and faithfulness of God. Indeed faith, where it exists at all, owes its very existence to some word of promise *given by God* in which we are led to trust; and therefore our faith, if we have any, is "the gift of God" (Eph. 2·8). We have only to read attentively the seventeenth and eighteenth chapters of Genesis to see that the bringing of Isaac into the world, with all that it meant to God and to us, was altogether the work of God; and that nature contributed nothing whatever to its accomplishment, but on the contrary presented obstacles thereto. It is evident that, for the carrying out of His purpose, God had not only to put forth that power which is His to quicken the dead, but had *first* to overcome the incredulity of Sarah's heart. In this we may find both instruction and encouragement. It should teach us to search our hearts for opposition to the implicit acceptance of the Word of God (see Heb. 3:7, 8, 13); and it should encourage us with the thought that God works even to overcome our natural disposition to doubt His Word and His faithfulness. Certainly God waited long, and had much to do in the heart of His hand-maiden Sarah, before she was brought to where she "judged Him faithful Who had promised."

In this connection we should give careful attention also to the corresponding account of Abraham's faith at that time, which account is found in Romans 4:13-22. Verses 20, 21 in the A. V. read thus: "He staggered not at the promise of God through unbelief: but was *strong in faith,* giving glory to God: and being fully persuaded that what He had promised He was able also to perform." We see then, that Abraham and Sarah both were brought into the

condition of counting trustfully on God to do "what He
had promised;" though it required many years to bring
them to that point, and though it had first to be made *impossible* for them to attain the desired end in their own
way, before they became willing to leave the accomplishment thereof entirely to God.

But the words "was strong in faith" would convey the
idea that the strength of *Abraham's faith* was a factor in
the work. That, however, is not the sense of the passage
at all; for the word rendered "strong" is a passive parti-
ciple meaning *empowered* or *made strong*. It is the same
word (only in verb form) as is used of Sarah—*"received*
strength." So the fact is, not that Abarham was strong
in faith—as if he had strength of faith in himself—but
that he was *made* strong *in* faith. It was *God* who
strengthened Abraham, and not his faith that did it. His
faith consisted simply in taking God at His word, and
thus making it possible for *God* to work out His own
purpose in His own way.

We trust our reader will not think we are giving too
much attention to the covenant which God made with
Abraham, as recorded in Genesis 17. It would indeed
be impossible for us to do so; for that covenant is the
basis of all God's dealings in grace for the working out of
His mighty purposes which He purposed in Christ Jesus
our Lord. That is the covenant represented by Sarah,
the first and the *true* wife; it is likened to a great mountain; it answers to the heavenly Jerusalem; its children
are born into liberty and are the heirs of God; and it is
expressly called the "Everlasting Covenant." Therefore
the subject is worthy of our best and most patient attention.

XII.

THE EVERLASTING COVENANT
(Heb. 13:20).

The two covenants referred to in Galatians 4 are usually spoken of as the "old" covenant and the "new" covenant; and it seems to be generally understood from those expressions that the covenant of the law was the first in point of time. Such however is not the case, since the covenant of grace, or "the promise," was made with Abraham and his seed, and is earlier than the law by more than four hundred years (Gal. 3:17). The covenant from Mount Sinai was the *first* to bring forth its appropriate results, and the *first* to run its course and grow "old"; but it was not the first in time. Corresponding to this is the fact that Abraham's marriage with Hagar was the first to bring forth its appropriate fruit, and to finish its course. But his marriage with Sarah was long before his relations with Hagar. These were but temporary; and they were broken off ere the true purpose of his union with Sarah was accomplished.

It is easy to identify "the everlasting covenant" by the fact that the expression occurs only once in the New Testament. The context in which it is found sheds clear light upon the entire subject we are studying. This is the familiar passage:

> "Now the God of peace that brought again from the dead our Lord Jesus, that great Shepherd of the sheep, *through the blood of the everlasting covenant,*

make you *perfect* in every good work to do His will, *working in you* that which is well-pleasing in His sight, through Jesus Christ, to Whom be glory forever. Amen" (Heb. 13:19, 20).

God is here presented as the God who *quickens the dead,* and the everlasting covenant is identified as that which was ratified in the blood of Jesus Christ and as that under which sins are forgiven and eternal life bestowed. The purpose of the covenant is declared by the words: "make you *perfect* in every good work to *do His will";* and the power for doing this is indicated by the clause, "working in you that which is well-pleasing in His sight through Jesus Christ." The correspondence with God's words to Abraham in Genesis 17:1 is complete. Abraham had long been a child of God by grace through faith, but he had yet to be made "perfect," to "walk" before God, through God's own power working in him.

The chief lesson from this portion of the Word of God to which we wish to call attention is that, while every believer in Jesus Christ is made, by regeneration of the Holy Ghost, a child of God, and hence is perfect as to his *standing in the family of God,* there is yet the need of a work (and it may be a long work) of the Spirit of God *in* him, to make him "perfect *in every good work* to do His (God's) will," and to make him *fruitful* to the glory of God through Jesus Christ. And with that goes the further lesson that the work of God in us may be hindered by our unwillingness to accept the decree of death to ourselves and our own wills, plans, and ways and to *trust God completely* for the doing of His own work in us and in His own way. Our own doings or "works" in the energy of the flesh, even though we may be thinking to accomplish results for God, may be simply hindering and delaying *His* working. Our part then is to *deny ourselves,* thus laying our own doings in the grave, to *take up our cross* daily, thus experiencing crucifixion to the world and to self as a part of our every day life, and to *follow Christ,* which is to "walk" before God and be "perfect." (Mat. 16:24, 25; Lu. 9:23-26). This was the secret of Paul's "walk" and of his fruitful service, as witnessed by the words "I by the law died to the law. I am crucified with Christ. Nevertheless I live; *yet not I,* but Christ liveth in me" (Gal. 2:19, 20). By the words "yet not I" Paul denied himself, thus fulfilling the Lord's conditions as to discipleship.

There is much valuable information about the everlasting covenant in the Epistle to the Hebrews, which we do not attempt to discuss in this present volume.* We would only point out here that what made the covenant of Mount Sinai "old" was not its antiquity, but the fact that God spoke through Jeremiah of making "a *new* covenant with the house of Israel and with the house of Judah." And in Hebrew 8:7-13 this interesting fact is stated, namely that "in that He saith, A *new* covenant, He hath made the first *old.*"

The covenant of Mt. Sinai was the first which God made *with the house of Israel.* The promise given through Jeremiah (Jer. 31:31-34) was simply a promise to establish with the house of Israel the ancient and everlasting covenant which He had first given to Abraham,

---

*See God's Pilgrims $1.00, and God's Apostle and High Priest 60c. Hamilton Bros., 120 Tremont St., Boston.

and concerning which He had said to him; "And I *will* establish My covenant between Me and thee and thy seed after thee *for an everlasting covenant*" (Gen. 17:7).

That covenant had stood unchanged and *unchangeable* (since God had given it *by promise* and not made it conditional on works of men) during all the period of the law; and under its terms all who believed in the God of Abraham, Isaac and Jacob, were saved by grace through faith. There never was salvation for sinners on any other basis; and on the other hand there never was a sinner of whatever nation who came, like Ruth, to trust in the living God, that did not find salvation through His mercy. The "everlasting covenant" remained in force during the episode or "parenthesis" of the law, just as Abraham's marriage relation with Sarah remained in force during his temporary conjugal relations with Hagar.

The everlasting covenant is mentioned in Psalm 105: 8-11, where we read: "Which covenant He made with Abraham, and His oath unto Isaac, and confirmed the same unto Jacob for an everlasting covenant." By this Scripture we learn that the land of Canaan was given to Israel, not under the covenant made at Mount Sinai, which covenant was immediately broken by them, but under the covenant of grace given to the fathers. This shows that that covenant was *always in force*. In fact God's dealings with Israel all the way from Egypt to Canaan, were in *grace* and in fulfilment of His promise to the fathers. The blood of the lamb was grace, and so was the way through the Red Sea, and the Pillar of Cloud and Fire, and the Smitten Rock, and the manna, and the Serpent lifted up. God says that "the people which were left of the sword found *grace* in the wilderness" (Jer. 31 : 2). But this is practically lost sight of in current teaching, which generally holds that the people found only *law* there.

But the everlasting covenant had never been "established" as a covenant to *"the house of Israel and house of Judah"* until Jesus Christ, the Mediator and Surety thereof, offered Himself as the Covenant-Victim (*diathemenos,* translated "testator" in Heb. 9 : 16, 17), and ratified it by His blood. By His death the everlasting covenant with its unspeakable benefits became effective to all the world. But, having been promised first to Israel, it must needs be proclaimed first to Israel. Hence the words of Peter: "Therefore let *all the house of Israel* know assuredly that God hath made that same Jesus, whom ye have crucified, both Lord and Christ" : and thereupon he preached to them repentance and the forgiveness of sins, and the gift of the Holy Ghost, in His Name. (Acts 2 : 36-39).

And in this connection we see special significance in the concluding words of Peter's address recorded in the next chapter of Acts, where he expressly mentioned *the covenant God made with Abraham,* and also the promises made through all the prophets from Samuel on, who never spake a word of setting up again the old broken covenant of Sinai, but always of a new order of things which Peter briefly describes by the comprehensive words "these days." We quote Acts 3 : 24-26:

> "Yea, and all the prophets from Samuel and those that follow after, as many as have spoken have likewise foretold of *these days.* Ye are the children of the prophets, and of *the covenant which God made*

with our fathers, saying unto Abraham, And in thy
Seed* shall *all the kindreds of the earth be blessed.*
Unto *you first"*—*i. e.* first of the kindreds of earth—
"God having raised up His Son Jesus sent Him to
bless you, in turning away everyone of you from his
iniquities."

There can therefore be no question as to what covenant
Peter was proclaiming, for it was that given to Abraham
and his Seed; nor can there be any doubt as to the nature
of the promised "blessing," for it consisted in turning
sinners away from their iniquities.

Moreover it was revealed both to Mary and to Zacha
rias at the very beginning of the dispensation, and was
declared in their inspired utterances, that what was then
at hand was the era of the fulfilment of God's promise to
Abraham.   Thus Mary said ·

"He hath holpen His servant Israel, in remembrance of His mercy, as He spake to our fathers, to
Abraham and to his Seed forever" (Luke 1: 52, 55).

And Zacharias said that God was about—

"To perform the mercy promised to our fathers,
and to *remember His holy covenant;* the *oath which
He sware to our father Abraham"* (Lu. 1: 72, 73)

Thus the mother of Jesus, and the father of John His
forerunner, were inspired to announce the approach of
the era of blessing to all nations through the promised
Seed of Abraham, and not, as some have mistakenly supposed, the approach of the era of Israel's earthly great-

---

*Singular number, meaning Christ, See Gal. 3:16, 19.

ness. These two prophecies, with that of the angel Gabriel to Zacharias (Lu. 1:13-17), are *the first words of God* breaking the long silence of four hundred years from Malachi. There can be no doubt that every word and act of God, beginning with the angel's message to Zacharias, belong to this present era which is the era of grace to all the world through Abraham's Seed. The "break" between the old dispensation and the new is a very wide one—over four hundred years. It occurs between the last word of Malachi and the first word of Matthew. Nevertheless some able commentators have failed to per ceive it, and have consequently sought to locate a dispensa tional "break," some at one place and some at another, subsequent to what is expressly called "The beginning of *the gospel of Jesus Christ the Son of God, as it is written in the prophets"* (Mk. 1:1, 2).

The next mention by name of the "everlasting covenant" is from the lips of David—which is very significant. The particular promises covenanted to Abraham were concerning the *family, the blessing,* and the *inheritance.* Nothing was said concerning the *throne.* That feature of the everlasting covenant was reserved to be disclosed in connection with David. For it is evident that the two pillars of the gospel-era are Abraham and David.

In the case of God's purposes for the throne we have dictinct foreshadowings in Saul and David, the former being the king according to the heart of man, as David was the king according to God's own heart. Thus, King Saul was to God's purpose for the throne what Ishmael was to His purposes for the family—nature's best, which must be tested, and proved to be unsuited to God's purposes, and be put out of the way ere God carries His will into effect.

The case of Saul and David not only foreshadows in a typical way the working out of God's purpose concerning the throne of the universe, but it also teaches for the individual saint a similar lesson to that taught by Ishmael and Isaac. The lesson is that we are all ruled at first by our own imperious wills, which are like King Saul, violent, erratic, impulsive, unstable, moody, sometimes giving way to gusts of temper, and sometimes displaying sentiment and religiousness. We must bring the dominion of self-rule to an end; we must dethrone Saul and *make David King,* that is to say, we must enthrone Christ in our hearts as Lord of all, before there can be any victory over our enemies or any peace within the realm of our own being.

The mention of the everlasting covenant by David is found in his "last words," wherein he said: "Although my house be not so with God, yet hath He made with me an *everlasting covenant,* ordered in all things and sure" (2 Sam. 23:5).

David's house was "not so with God," that is, not what God required of His royal house; for the house of David ended in complete failure, after a period counted by God as fourteen generations. (Mat. 1:6-11). But God's everlasting covenant is not affected in the least by the failure of those to whom it is given. Being dependent upon *His faithfulness alone,* it is sure to be fulfulled by Him. God gave His word to Abraham concerning his posterity and their inheritance, and confirmed it with an oath (see Heb. 6:17, 20). Likewise concerning David it is written:

"I have made a covenant with My chosen, I have sworn unto David My servant, Thy seed will I establish forever, and build up thy throne to all generations" (Psa. 89: 3, 4).

It is clear from the New Testament Scriptures that, as God's promise to Abraham concerning the inheritance and the blessing was far greater than appeared by the record in Genesis, so His promise to David and his Seed concerning the throne is far greater than appeared by the Old Testament. But we do not pursue that part of the everlasting covenant, for Galatians is not concerned with the throne.

The next mention of the everlasting covenant is in Isaiah, where we have the words ·

"Incline your ear, and come unto Me: hear, and your soul shall live; and I will make an *everlasting covenant with you,* even the sure mercies of David" (Isa. 55: 3).

This prophecy is unmistakably a promise whereof the fulfilment belongs to this present gospel-era; and it is specially pertinent because it is a part of the same passage from which Paul quotes in the "allegory" of Galatians 4, where he applies the words, "Rejoice thou barren that bearest not" to the heavenly Jerusalem, to which the new covenant pertains. This confirms the truth that the blessing of the "everlasting covenant" given to Abraham and his Seed and to David and his Seed are "the unsearchable riches of Christ," preached to Jew and Gentile alike during the present dispensation. Those blessings are, moreover, called "the sure mercies of David."

But we do not inquire here into the significance of that expression.

The "everlasting covenant" is again mentioned by name in the chapter from which the Lord read and on which He based His address in the synagogue at Nazareth (Isaiah 61)

In Jeremiah 32:37-41, in a prophecy which speaks of the gathering of Israel out of all countries whither they have been driven, we read this promise:

"And they shall be My people, and I will be their God: And I will give them one heart and one way, that they may fear Me forever for the good of them and of their children after them: And I will make an *everlasting covenant* with them that I will not turn away from them to do them good; but I will put My fear in their hearts, that they shall not depart from Me."

The passage follows close upon the promise of the New Covenant (Jer. 31:31-34), to which we have already referred: and it shows that, being accepted of God on the ground of redemption, Israel will never depart from Him again.

The same promise in substance is found in Ezekiel 16:60·

"Nevertheless, I will remember My covenant with thee in the days of thy youth, and I will establish unto thee an *everlasting covenant.*"

In Ezekiel 37, following the vision of the dry bones (which we believe is fulfilled in God's spiritual Israel of this dispensation and will have a further fulfilment in the earthly nation hereafter), is a remarkable passage in which Christ is referred to as "David." We quote:

> "And David My servant shall be King over them; and they all shall have one Shepherd; they shall also walk in My judgments, and observe My statutes to do them. * * And My servant David shall be their Prince forever. Moreover, I will make a *covenant of peace* with them; it shall be an *everlasting covenant* with them" (Ezek. 37:24-28).

There is a marked correspondence between this passage and that in Hebrews 13:19, 20, where God is called "the God of *peace*" and Christ is named "the great Shepherd of the sheep" and His blood is spoken of as "the blood of the everlasting covenant." Especially we call attention to the words: "They shall also observe My statutes, and walk in My judgments to do them," which declare what is ever the purpose of God in His people. To this we find the response in the great passage in Hebrews 13:20, 21, in the words: "Working in you that which is well pleasing in His sight," which means *obedience to His Word*.

From all the foregoing Scriptures we gather that the "everlasting covenant" in all its breadth, embracing God's promises to both Abraham and David, is nothing less than the declaration, in the form of a Covenant which carries with it an obligation to fulfil all its terms, of God's eternal purpose which He purposed in Christ Jesus concerning His own family—the "many sons" whom He is "bringing unto glory"; concerning the earth also, and the nations thereof, among whom the earthly Israel is to have the foremost place. Hence the purposes concerning Israel, which under the covenant of Mount Sinai were condi tional upon their obedience, become unconditional under the everlasting covenant, which precedes the other and stands forever. For that covenant is represented by "Mount Zion which cannot be removed, but abideth forever" (Psa. 125:1).

Upon close examination of the foregoing Scriptures it will appear, we think, that so much of the everlasting covenant as was pledged to David—in other words that part of it which embraces the throne—is confined to God's people *of this dispensation.* The blessings of eternal life, and a share in the inheritance, which appear in God's promises to Abraham, will undoubtedly be the portion of the saved nation of Israel in the future. But, among the promises to "the house of Israel and house of Judah" in Jeremiah, there is no suggestion of sharing the throne. "The sure mercies of David," which embrace the promise of reigning with Christ, if so be that we *suffer with Him* (Rom. 8:17; 2 Tim. 2:12), belong exclusively to the gospel of this dispensation. For there will be no opportunity to suffer with Christ in the age to come.

We can see in this a reason why the promises concerning the throne were separated from the other promises of the everlasting covenant, and were pledged to David's Son, not to Abraham's. For while all David's seed are the seed of Abraham, not all Abraham's seed are the seed of David. We can see in this also, why David is the first of the fathers to be mentioned by name in the New Testament, and why Paul connects the gospel more prominently with David than with Abraham.

XIII

THE TWO SONS
(Gal. 4:22).

It is evident that the two sons stand for two lines of posterity. Both these lines of descent proceeded from Abraham, the man of faith, yet between them there is a difference as great as that between bondage and liberty, between a nation of bondmen and a nation of freemen. Specifically, Ishmael stands for "Israel after the flesh" (1 Cor. 10:18), the natural descendants of Jacob, while Isaac stands for the spiritual people of God, the household of faith, "the Israel of God." Both, we say, could equally claim Abraham as their father; and Ishmael had the prior claim by fourteen years, during which time he was the *only* child of Abraham, and also the heir-apparent of the promise. But the great difference between the two is that Ishmael was born "after the flesh," whereas Isaac was supernaturally born, "after the Spirit." Isaac was, in one word, a miracle, and so is *everyone* that is born of the Spirit.

There was a brief time (from the birth of Isaac until he was weaned) during which the two sons lived under the same roof; and it is written that, during that time, "he that was born after the flesh persecuted him that was born after the Spirit" (Gal. 4:29). This is applied for us by the brief comment, "Even so it is now." The apostle applied the illustration primarily to the persecution being then carried on by the Jews, the earthly Israel, against the saints, the true Israel. Paul had been the the leader of this persecution, but now he had become the chief sufferer from it. Was he proving in that way the truth of what he declared in chapter 6:7, that "Whatso ever a man soweth *that* shall he also reap"?

But the illustration of the two sons of Abraham reaches much farther than that. It applies to a situation which ever confronts the spiritual seed of Abraham. It is a situation out of which persecution is sure to arise if they refuse to conform to the desires of the flesh and the ways of the world in regard to religious customs and observances, particularly the observance of so called "holy days," and seasons, such as the "Christmas season."

What should be impressed upon us first of all is the sharp line of separation which the Word of God draws between all that Ishmael stands for and all that Isaac stands for. This difference teaches us that we should keep ourselves "free" from everything that is of the works of the flesh, and particularly its religious works. Those things are absolutely foreign to us who are the children of promise. They belong exclusively to the children of the bondwoman. To adopt them, therefore, or to take part in them, is to *deny our heavenly birth and our citizenship in the New Jerusalem,* which is "free," and to surrender the liberty we have in Christ, wherewith He has "made us free" through His death on the cross.

When Christ came to the nation Israel, there were in the mass of that nation many Ishmaels and a few Isaacs. But they were not separated; for *all* counted· themselves Abraham's seed, and boasted of it (John 8:33). But now there was to be a separation. For the Isaacs were to come out from among the Ishmaels, and the Ishmaels were to be "cast out" (Mat. 8:12). Those who heard the voice of the Son of God and believed on Him were "Isaacs." They came out from the great mass of "Ishmaels" and followed Him. The little remnant (represented by Isaac) who repented at the preaching of John the Baptist, and so were "prepared for the Lord," *received Him,* and to them He gave power to become the children of God; for they were the true seed of Abraham (John 1:10-13). It is important to see that John's ministry had reference to this very matter. For he warned the Pharisees and Sadducees, saying: "Bring forth fruits meet for repentance, and think not to say within yourselves, We have Abraham to our father" (Mat. 3:8, 9).

The lesson unfolded for us by Paul in Galatians was briefly taught by the Lord in one of His discussions with the Scribes and Pharisees. He had given "to those Jews which believed on Him" the promise: "If ye continue in My Word, then are ye My disciples indeed; and ye shall know the truth, and the truth shall make you free" (John 8:31, 32).

What the Lord meant by "the truth" is undoubtedly the full "truth of the Gospel" as unfolded in the New Testament, that is to say "the law of the Spirit of life in Christ Jesus" which makes *"free* from the law of *sin* and death." But the scribes and Pharisees objected to that saying of the Lord, and answered Him: "We be Abraham's seed, and were never in bondage to any man: how sayest thou, Ye shall be made free"? The Lord's reply shows that He was speaking of spiritual bondage, that of sin, and of the spiritual freedom from the dominion of sin, which He alone can give, and which the children of God alone possess. Jesus answered them, "Verily, verily

I say unto you, whosoever committeth sin is the servant (bond slave) of sin. And the servant abideth not in the house forever: but the Son abideth ever. If the Son therefore shall make you free, ye shall be free indeed."

It is easy to see in these words a reference to the same truth which is illustrated in the allegory of Galatians 4. The "son" of the house abideth in it, as did Isaac the true son and heir of his father. But the servant has no title to be there, and may be cast out, as was Ishmael.

In the verses that follow we find the clear distinction, to which we have been calling attention, between Abraham's descendants after the flesh, and the true children of Abraham, that is, those who are of the *faith* of Abraham. For the Lord said to them: "I know that ye are Abraham's seed; but ye seek to kill Me, because My word hath no place in you." (v. 37). Thus He acknowledged them to be the natural descendants of Abraham. But He immediately added: "If ye were Abraham's *children, ye* would do *the works of Abraham,"* that is to say works of *faith* (v. 38).

There is also here a lesson for us as individuals. For inasmuch as we who are of the faith of Jesus Christ are the children of Abraham *not by the bond woman but by the free woman,* we ought to give careful attention to the lesson which this illustration has for us personally. We have each in the house of our mortal body an Ishmael— the old man—and also an Isaac—the new man. That which was born of the flesh was, prior to our conversion, the only occupant of the premises, and hence he had the full and undisputed use of our members. During that time we had certain religious sentiments (stronger with some than with others), and these we sought to satisfy by engaging in dead religious works, going to church, taking part in "services," keeping days, receiving the "sacrament," and the like. Not only are these "works" the things to which the old nature (Ishmael) instinctively turns for the satisfaction of its religious yearnings, or in the attempt to quiet a troublesome conscience, but the fact is, that there is nothing else to which it can resort for such purposes. Hence God gave certain religious observances to "Israel after the flesh," but they were to serve only a fleshly purpose—"to the purifying of *the flesh*" (Heb. 9:13)—and they were parts of a *temporary* sys tem, which was to last only "until the time of reforma tion" (Heb. 9:10-11)—that is, till Christ should come.

But, when all these religious works proved to be vain, and when, awakened through the gospel, we sought God's mercy freely offered in Christ Jesus—then a *new creature* came into existence. Isaac was born in our heart; and for a time it was all "laughter," the joy of the first dawning consciousness of salvation full and free through the atoning blood of Jesus Christ. We thus fulfilled Sarah's prophecy when she said: "All *that hear* will laugh with me" (Gen. 21:6). But Ishmael was not by any means disposed to vacate the premises, nor to yield up to the new-comer the use of the members of the mortal body. Hence there ensued a struggle, answering to the persecution which little Isaac endured at the hands of his older half-brother. We found indeed that "that which is born of the flesh *is* flesh," and that it cannot be changed into something different. We found also that, if we had to fight it out alone, the flesh would invariably get the better of us. But it is in view of this very need (amongst other purposes) that God has given His Holy

Spirit to dwell in us. This is the meaning of verses 16 and 17 of chapter 5·

> "I say then, Walk in the Spirit, and ye shall not fulfil the lust of the flesh. For the flesh lusteth against (or has desires contrary to) the Spirit, and the Spirit against the flesh; and these are *contrary* the one to the other; so that ye cannot do the things that ye would."

It is only through the Spirit then that we can successfully oppose the flesh. Merely to set our own wills against the cravings of the flesh, even when those cravings are recognized as both sinful and also dangerous to health and even life—is vain. Sometimes the conflict is indeed a matter of *life* and *death*. Thus in Romans 8:13 it is written: "For if ye (children of God) live after the flesh, ye shall die; but if ye through the Spirit do put to death the deeds of the body, ye shall live."

The writer has proved the truth of these Scriptures more than once in his experiences. For example, and as a pertinent illustration, he would mention that in his unconverted days he was in bondage to the habit of smoking, and though he made many efforts, even putting forth all his will-power, he could not escape from that bondage. The last human physician he ever consulted about his health told him that he *must* give up smoking, as his heart was seriously affected; but the best he could do was to desist for a few days. Some months later, however, when as a "new creature in Christ Jesus," he came to see that the habit was grieving to God's Spirit, he found strength in *less than one moment,* "through the Spirit," to put that habit to death, and was delivered instantly and permanently from even the desire to indulge in what had been for many years a necessity. That was more than sixteen years ago. "Therefore we are *not* debtors to the flesh to live after the flesh"; for there is *no need* that a child of God, having the Spirit of God as his "Comforter" (*One at hand to help,* is what the word signifies), should be "in bondage" to any form of fleshly gratification.

The words of 2 Cor. 3:17, may be fittingly referred to in this connection. The passage in which they occur is like that of Galatians 4, a comparison (though with a view to different aspects of the matter) between the two covenants. Here we see again that the covenant of law is characterized by *bondage, condemnation* and *death;* whereas the covenant of grace is characterized by *righteousness, life* and *liberty.* The passage contains, near the end, these words: "Now the Lord is that Spirit: and where the Spirit of the Lord is, there is *liberty."* Thus the thought of *liberty* is specially associated with the Spirit.

The special "liberty" spoken of in the passage quoted from 2 Corinthians, is deliverance from the blinding power of darkness; so that we, contemplating and reflecting as in a mirror the glory of the Lord, revealed in the Scriptures, are being changed into the same image *from* glory (seen *in Him* its Source) *to glory,* as wrought by the power of the Spirit, *in us.* The passage also indicates a progressive advance in conformity to the image of Christ, as from one degree of glory to another.

This lesson is exceedingly practical, and is of precious value.

But there is more to be learned by us for our individual profit, from the allegory of the two sons of Abraham.

The spiritual children of Abraham are liable to exhibit the traits of their father in *repeating the things done by him which were not of faith.* Thus we find Isaac practising the same deception his father had practised, in pretending that Rebekah was his sister, and not his wife (Gen. 26:7). So we need to be watchful against the treachery and deception of our natural hearts. What is particularly to be noticed in the case of the Hagar episode is that it was a plan *suggested by Sarah* (which would naturally have commended it to Abraham), and was adopted by him *for the purpose of accomplishing the revealed will of God.* We may be sure also that Abraham "prayed about it," which often is made to take the place of obedience to the written Word, especially when some cherished plan of our own is in view—it may be even in connection with the work of the Lord. It is easier and more natural to "pray about it" and go our own way, than to follow the Word of the Lord. But our lesson plainly teaches us that, although a plan may be suggested by one whose opinion we value, even by a beloved wife—and though it may be devised for the accomplishment of some known purpose of God—and although He may not interfere, but allow it, so far as appearances go, to *succeed* —yet it may serve not to advance His object, but to retard it. In all such cases we will find that the outcome of our well-laid plans and painstaking efforts is, after all only an "Ishmael."

"He that *believeth* shall not make haste" (Isa. 28:16). Hence in making haste to accomplish some good end, we may be acting not in faith, but in the flesh. Here again the help of the Spirit is needed to overcome and restrain the impulsiveness of the flesh, and to enable us to *wait* until God's full time comes, and *then* we will see His object accomplished *in His own way,* not at all through our efforts, but through ourselves as *instruments in His hands.* For we need the Spirit of God not only to enable us to put to death the doings of the body, and to walk in God's ways, and to bring forth fruit, but also to *wait.* "For we *through the Spirit* do *wait* for the hope of righteousness *by faith"* (5:5).

Looking now to a broader application of our illustration, it is easy to see that it strikingly corresponds with the situation in which the household of faith, as a whole, finds itself at the present time. There is a clear resemblance between Ishmael and nominal Christianity. Christendom claims Abraham for its father, so to speak; and, indeed, in a sense, it *is* derived from the same sources as true Christianity. However, it was born, as it were, of the Egyptian woman—the world. And just as Isaac was daily confronted by his big brother Ishmael (until the bond-woman and her son were finally "cast out"), even so the weak little company of true believers is in contact hourly with the great modern Christendom and her chil dren, who are "in bondage" to systems of religious rites and ceremonies, especially the observance of days ("Easter," "Christmas," etc.), and seasons ("Lent, "Advent," etc.), to which the more religiously-minded attach great importance. There is, therefore, that ever present danger of slipping into these forbidden ways; and hence we should give heed to the exhortation that bids us "Stand fast in the liberty wherewith Christ has made us free, and not be entangled *again* with the yoke of bondage" (5:1).

Great help in the interpretation of this allegory is found in verse 27, which is quoted from the first verse of Isaiah 54. This tells us that the grand prophecy of that chapter refers to the true Israel, which represents also the Jerusalem above, which is free, and is "the mother of us all." This surely is of the deepest interest; but since we have given some thoughts about the prophecy of Isaiah 54 in other writings, our present comments will be brief.

In view of the parallel expressions "Abraham, who is the *father of us all*" (Rom. 4: 16) and "Jerusalem which is above * * * which is the *mother of us all*" (Gal. 4: 26, 27), it is of great interest to know that Abraham was looking for the City which has the glorious foundations described in this prophecy, which City is the final outlook of all the household of faith. (Comp. Isa. 54:11, 12, Heb. 11:10; Rev. 21:19, 20)

Isaiah 53 contains the foretelling of the sufferings, death and burial of Christ (verses 4-9), and in this connection the question is asked: "Who shall declare His generation? For He was *cut off* out of the land of the living." Being thus "cut off" without any to succeed to His Name (cf. Dan. 9:26), who shall declare His generation? But, notwithstanding that He was "cut off," verse 10 contains the clear promise: "*He shall see His seed.*" And in the next chapter we have, in glowing prophecy, the new family—mother and children—the Lord Himself, the Redeemer, being the "Husband."

The history of this desolate woman, now become the mother of a great family, corresponds wonderfully with that of Sarah. Sarah was barren and did not bear. That was "the shame of her youth." There was also "the reproach of her widowhood," this expression being a reference to the time when Hagar was the actual wife of Abraham (referred to in quotation in Gal. 4 : 27, as "she which hath the husband"). Then, in Sarah's old age, there was the intervention of the Lord "with great mercies" resulting in "Laughter," insomuch that the shame of her youth was forgotten and the reproach of her widowhood not remembered any more.

Not only so, but the children of this desolate one who became, when past all hope, the subject of God's rich mercies, were to be "more than the children of the married wife."

Moreover, in verse 10 God's "covenant" is mentioned, and although the word "everlasting" is not used in that verse (it is found in chapter 55 : 3), the covenant is said to be stedfast as the hills. Hence it is easy to trace the application of the prophecy to this dispensation. The believing remnant of Israel which repented at the preaching of John the Baptist, is represented by Sarah as a type, and by the desolate woman of Isaiah 54 as a prophetic symbol. At the time of Christ's coming, Israel was old, barren, "as good as dead," and past all hope of bringing forth fruit for God. There were a few *individual believers* among the mass of Israel, but no *family*, no "household of faith," distinct from the nation as a whole. But, after the resurrection of Christ, the Spirit comes down, quickening those who repent and believe, giving birth through the gospel to the "many sons" whom God is now bringing unto glory, and uniting them into a distinct family ("the household of God").

Then began, also, the "casting out" of those born after the flesh. This, with the simultaneous *bringing in* of Gentile believers, was foretold by the Lord in one of His first prophetic utterances when, in commending the faith of the Gentile centurion, He said:

> "Verily I say unto you, I have not found so great faith, no, not in Israel. And I say unto you that many shall come from the east and west, and sit down with Abraham and Isaac and Jacob" (the stock or trunk of the olive tree) "in the Kingdom of heaven, but the children of the kingdom shall be *cast out* into outer darkness" (Mat. 8:10-12).

Peter also, in addressing the multitude in Jerusalem after the healing of the impotent man, referred to the casting out of unbelieving Jews. For after quoting God's promise through Moses, of the coming of a special "Prophet," Peter said:

> "And it shall come to pass that every soul which will not hear *that Prophet* shall be *destroyed from among the people*" (Acts 3:23).

This same truth is plainly taught by Paul also in the illustration of the olive tree, found in Romans 11:16-32. In studying this illustration it should be noticed that the subject of the passage is the *true* "Israel" (here called the "remnant according to the election of grace," v. 5). Paul is distinguishing this "remnant," which answers to Isaac, from the mass of unconverted Israelites, answering to Ishmael. The nation *in its entirety* is likened to an olive tree, whereof Abraham is the root. But many of "the branches," representing the unbelieving members of the house of Israel, were "broken off" (v. 17). This word "broken off" corresponds to the "cast out" of Mat. 8:12, and of Gal. 4:30, and the "destroyed" of Acts 3:23. The

"breaking off" of the *"natural* branches" (v. 24), that is
to say, of the unbelieving Israelites whose eyes were
blinded and whose hearts were hardened, left only the
spiritual branches, the believing Israelites, joined to the
stock of the olive tree (See Jer. 11 : 16, 17). But now a
marvellous thing happens—a thing which indeed was always part of God's great plan of redemption, but which
had been hidden in previous ages and therefore is called
a "mystery," namely this, that believing *Gentiles,* are
now "graffed in among" the natural olive branches and
are made to partake of the *root* and *fatness* of the olive
tree.

Thus "the Israel of God" is constituted by means of
two distinct operations. The first is the *cutting off* of
those Israelites who refuse Christ; and the second is the
adding of those from among the Gentiles who accept
Christ when presented to them by the gospel.

We have said that the "root" of the olive tree represents Abraham. The "fatness" (or richness) thereof represents the "Blessing" promised through Abraham, which
is first of all *Christ,* and the *Holy Spirit* Who is given by
and through Christ. We have seen that "the blessing of
Abraham" is the Spirit (Gal. 3 : 14) ; and, moreover, the
olive, from which the oil is produced, is emblematic of
Christ giving the Holy Spirit to those "who are of the
household of faith" (Gal. 6 : 10).

The word "partakest of" in Romans 11 : 17, is also instructive and helpful in guiding us to the meaning of this
passage. All believers partake of "the root," for all are
the children of Abraham, who is "the father of us all."
They "partake" also of all the promises, particularly "the

promise in Christ" (Eph. 3:6-8), and "the promise of
the Spirit" (Gal. 3:14). Thus we read in Hebrews 4:14,
"For we are made *partakers of Christ,* if we hold the be-
ginning of our confidence stedfast to the end" (as every
real child of Abraham will do); and in Hebrews 6:4,
"Who were once enlightened, and have tasted of the
Heavenly Gift, and were made *partakers of the Holy
Ghost.*"*

The "mystery" which in other ages was not made known
by revelation of God unto the sons of men, but which
"is now revealed unto His holy apostles and prophets† by
the Spirit" (Eph. 3:5), has to do with the partaking by
Gentiles, equally with believing Jews, in "the unsearchable
riches of Christ."   It is easy to see that the figure of the
olive tree wonderfully illustrates this truth; for, as both
the natural branches and the grafted-in branches partake
equally of the life of the tree, so believing Jews and believing Gentiles are equally the members of Christ, partaking equally of His life, and of the same Holy Spirit
(Eph. 2:14, 15).

An important detail of "this mystery" is stated in
Romans 11:25, 26, namely, that the present blindness (or

---

*This *passage refers to believers.* The word "enlightened" means only
one thing, and it is impossible to apply it to those who are in nature's
darkness. Only those who have been born again have been "enlightened,"
have "tasted of the Heavenly Gift," God's living Bread (John 6:32), and
have been made "partakers of the Holy Ghost." There are many reasons
why these will never "fall away," and one of those reasons is that, if they
should do so, it would be impossible to renew them again unto repentance." Mere "professors" (to whom this passage is sometimes applied)
may "fall away" from their empty profession (as the present writer did)
and yet may be brought to repentance. But that would not be a "re-
newing"; for the renewal here spoken of is the new birth which can happen
only once in any man's experience. For an explanation of this· interesting
passage see God's Pilgrims, Revised Ed., chap. 10.

---

†Not to Paul only or even primarily, but to *all* the apostles and New
Testament prophets, and to some before Paul was converted.

hardness) which has happened in part to Israel (*i. e.,* to the part that believes not), is to last only "until the fulness of the Gentiles be come in." For then "There shall come out of Sion the Deliverer, and shall turn away ungodliness from Jacob" (v. 26).

Thus we see that "the bond-woman and her son"—the house of Israel after the flesh—are "cast out," having no part or share in the present "Blessing," the Holy Spirit, or in the coming "Inheritance." For thus it is written to Gentiles who believe in Christ:

> "In Whom, having believed, ye were sealed with that *Holy Spirit of Promise*: Who is the Earnest of our inheritance until the *redemption of the purchased possession*" (Eph. 1:13, Gr.; see also Eph. 4:30).

In this "Blessing" and "Promise," believing Gentiles share with believing Jews; and on the other hand unbelieving Jews equally with unbelieving Gentiles are shut out. The former are *cast* out, and the latter are *left* out.

XIV.

THE TWO MOUNTAINS: THE TWO CITIES

"For the LORD hath chosen Zion; He hath desired it for His habitation This is my rest forever; here will I dwell" (Psa. 132:13, 14).

In the passage we are studying only one of the mountains is named. We read that one covenant was from the Mount Sinai, which covenant brings forth into bondage, and is represented by Hagar. We read further that Hagar answereth to Jerusalem which now is, and is in bondage with her children. The truth of this part of the Scripture stands vividly before our eyes as we contemplate the sad condition of unbelieving Israel at the present time. For theirs is truly a state of "bondage" to dense spiritual darkness. Thus they are, all unconsciously to themselves, a witness to all men of the truth of the prophetic Scripture. Those among them who attempt to maintain their ancient religion have only the corpse of Judaism. They have to content themselves with pitiful makeshifts in lieu of the sacrifices and ceremonies prescribed for them by the law of Moses. For the essence of Judaism is the *Altar;* and the appointed place of the altar and of all Jewish ceremonial, is Jerusalem. But temple, altar, sacrifice, priesthood, and holy days—all have been swept away. Nevertheless, the rags of the ancient ritual remain in the observance, after a fashion, of "days, and months, and times, and years"; and not only so, but even those from among the Gentiles who profess Christ manifest a desire for these "weak and beggarly elements," being more than willing to be brought again into bondage thereto.

Although no mention is made in our passage of the other mountain, there is mention of the other *city*—Jerusalem, which is above; and from that and other indications we have no difficulty in connecting the everlasting covenant with *Mount Zion*. In fact, the Epistle to the Hebrews, wherein the truth concerning the two covenants is unfolded at length, contains this plain statement

> "For ye are not come unto the mount that might be touched (Mount Sinai), and that burned with fire, nor unto blackness and darkness and tempest, and the sound of the trumpet, and the voice of words * * But ye *are* come unto MOUNT ZION, and unto THE CITY OF THE LIVING GOD, THE HEAVENLY JERUSALEM" (Heb. 12:17, 24).

This passage tells us quite clearly what system of things we *have not* come to, and what we *have* come to. The two systems referred to, with their various features, were both appointed by God Himself. One was appointed for the dispensation of law; the other for the dispensation of grace. Though both were from God, His Word distinguishes sharply between them. Hence it causes confusion to bring over things which pertained exclusively to Mount Sinai, and connect them with Mount Zion. There is a designed and manifest correspondence between the earthly Jerusalem and the heavenly Jerusalem. But *they belong to different worlds.* Our spiritual citizenship, which involves our allegiance and all our political relationships, is in the heavenly City, not in the earthly. This is not mysticism, nor a figure of speech. It is simple, sober *truth*,. to be apprehended by faith, and is of great practical value. Many troublesome questions can be settled for us by simply remembering that "our citizenship is in heaven, from whence also we look for the Saviour" (Phil. 3:20, 21).

When we begin to seek the spiritual significance of Mount Zion, and Jerusalem, we find ourselves led into rich truth having many features of deepest interest. Into all this we have no thought of entering at present. What is immediately connected with the subject brought before us in Galatians is that *"Zion" stands for the dwelling-place of God,* and that "Jerusalem" is *the city of the Great King;* as it is written:

> "Great is the LORD and greatly to be praised, in *the city of our God,* in *the mountain of His holiness.* Beautiful for situation, the joy of the whole earth, is *Mount Zion,* on the sides of the north, the City of *the Great King"* (Psa. 48:1, 2).

The Lord Jesus uses the same expression when He for bids the citizens of His heavenly kingdom to take oaths (a commandment many of them ignore and disobey), saying:

> *"Swear not at all;* neither by heaven, for it is God's throne; nor by the earth, for it is His footstool; neither by Jerusalem, for it is *the City of the Great King"* (Mat. 5:30, 36).

It is good indeed to know that we are not come to Mount Sinai; but let us not forget that we *are* come to Mount Zion, and to the heavenly Jerusalem, the City of

the Great King, Who now is crowned in heaven, and
Who has left us His commandments, which we are to
keep—yes, even to "the least" of them (Mat. 5:19), for
His glory, for our present good and eternal reward, and
to show thereby our love for Him (John 14:15, 21, 23;
15:10).

Particular heed should be given to the fact that the
lesson based upon the truth that we are come to Mount
Zion, and to what is divinely associated with that Mount,
is declared in the words: "See that ye refuse not Him that
speaketh." Manifestly, what is suited to the dwelling-
place of God is perfect submission to His revealed will.
The heavenly Jerusalem is the abiding-place of "the household of faith," also called "the Israel of God." They are
in the Kingdom of heaven, and their house is in the
Heavenly City. Hence they are under the rule of the
King of heaven, "the King invisible" (1 Tim. 1:17). Not
only so, but they are of *the King's own family*. Hence
their submission should be the *willing* submission of *children,* not the *enforced* submission of *subjects.* There is
no compulsion for them, no tribunals to try their wrong
doings and to decree penalties for their transgressions.
They are under a Father's government, and are subject to
a *Father's* chastening (Heb. 12:5, 11). But while there
are no prescribed pains and penalties for specific violations
of the laws of the Kingdom of heaven on the part of those
who, by grace, enjoy its unspeakable blessings, nevertheless *momentous consequences hinge upon their obedience.*
"For if *they* escaped not who refused him who spake on
earth (Moses), *much more* shall not we escape if we turn
away from Him Who speaketh from heaven" (Heb.
12:25).

Many are the Scriptures which declare that Zion is the chosen dwelling-place of God, and the royal city of the Heavenly Kingdom. Zion comes first into view in connection with David, who after reigning seven years in Hebron, went to Jerusalem with his men, and took it from the Jebusites, though the latter had deemed that to be as impossible a feat as to perform the miracle of taking the lame and the blind away. *"Nevertheless, David took the stronghold of Zion:* the same is the city of David" (2 Sam. 5:4-7).

In the Second Psalm we have that great prophecy which points in a special way to this age of the Gospel, because in it the Lord is called "the Son" (verses 7 and 12), and also the "Anointed," or "Christ" (v. 2). The rejection of God's Anointed One by the concerted action of rulers and peoples is foretold in verses 1-3. Then heaven's response to their rejection of Christ is foretold in the words:

"Yet have I set My King upon Zion the hill of My holiness." (v. 6.)

This points to the present era during which Christ is enthroned in heaven, and the kings and rulers of earth are admonished to submit to Him. Moreover, the gospel is declared in the words: "Blessed are all they that put their trust in Him." The coming age is also foretold, when His wrath will be kindled, and when He shall ask, and God shall give Him the nations for His inheritance, and the uttermost parts of the earth for His possession.

The 125th Psalm speaks, in words appropriate to quote in this connection, of the security of those who trust in the Lord:

"They that trust in the Lord shall be as MOUNT ZION, which cannot be removed, but abideth for ever. As the mountains are round about Jerusalem, so the LORD is round about His people from henceforth even for ever" (Ps. 125:12; comp. in Heb. 12:28, the words: "We receiving a kingdom which cannot be moved").

We quote also from Psalm 48:

"As we have heard, so have we seen in the city of the LORD of Hosts, in the city of our God: God will establish it forever. Selah" (v. 8).

It is given us even now to see by faith that heavenly Zion, whereof glorious things are spoken, the City of our God, so wonderfully described in the last two chapters of the Bible. The closing verses of this Psalm tell of the loving interest which those, whose affections are set on things above, take in God's City, even though the kings of the earth are troubled by the sight thereof, and hasten away (see verses 4-5):

"Let Mount Zion rejoice, let the daughters of Judah be glad, because of Thy judgments. Walk about Zion, and go round about her; tell the towers thereof, mark ye well her bulwarks, consider her palaces, that ye may tell it to the generation following" (v. 12, 13).

Many other Scriptures will be found to be rich in meaning for us if we read them with the thought in mind that Zion is God's dwelling-place, chosen for Himself, and for

the household of the many sons whom He is bringing unto
glory.

We refer to one more prophecy, which has an important bearing on our subject.   It is Psalm 133:

"Behold, how good and how pleasant it is   for
brethren to dwell together in unity.   It is like the
precious ointment upon the head, that ran down upon
the beard, even Aaron's beard; that went down to the
skirts of his garments; as the dew of Hermon, and
as the dew that descended upon the mountains of
Zion, for *there* the LORD commanded *the blessing,*
even *life forevermore.*"

A beautiful symbolic picture is this, presenting Christ
and all His members sharing the anointing for God's eternal Priesthood, their anointing being symbolized by that
wonderful and fragrant ointment, which was reserved for
God's own appointed use, and which it was death to imitate (Ex. 30:23-33).   When applied to the head it produced a cloud of fragrance, which gradually enveloped the
entire person of Aaron, the high-priest.

We find the counterpart of this in the few words of II
Corinthians 1:21, 22:

"Now He which stablisheth us (believing Jews)
with you (believing Gentiles, making up the royal
and priestly family) and *hath anointed* us, is God;
Who hath also sealed us, and given the Earnest of the
Spirit in our hearts."

All "brethren" share together *"the blessing,"* which is

the Spirit, imparting "life forevermore"; and what is of special interest is that the unity of the Spirit, in which brethren are to dwell, is likened also to "the dew that de scended upon Mount Zion," whereof it is said that "THERE the Lord commanded *the blessing,* even *life forevermore."*

Having *that* life then, which is shared by all God's chil dren, *how are we to live it?* All that is put before us in this Epistle, as well as in other portions of the Word, leads up to that question.   And all our studies of these wonderful things will profit us only to the extent we *put into practice* the things that pertain to the life which has been imparted to us. The question may be put in this way: By what *law* are we to live while here on earth awaiting translation to our heavenly home? The answer is given us with all the clearness that could be desired: we are to live by "the law of Christ," or as it is described in Romans 8:2, by "the law of the Spirit of life in Christ Jesus." Into that important subject we purpose to look more closely in the pages which follow,

XV.

THE YOKE OF BONDAGE
(Gal. 5:1).

The conclusion and climax of the remarkable allegory of Chapter 4 is given in these words: "So then, brethren, we are not children of the bondwoman, but of the free." In verse 28 it is said: "Now we, brethren, as Isaac was, are the children of promise." And to this the next verse adds the statement that we are born "after the Spirit."

Upon these strong and clear statements is based the exhortation: "Stand fast therefore in the liberty wherewith Christ hath made us free, and be not entangled again with the yoke of bondage." This Scripture reminds us that we owe our freedom to Christ; and it reminds us also of the great price, His own life, which He paid to make us free. For it takes us back to the beginning of the Epistle, where the foundation for the special lesson it enforces is laid in the words: "Our Lord Jesus Christ, Who *gave Himself* for our sins, that He might deliver us from (or out of) this present evil world." A freedom procured for us by our blessed Lord, and at so great a cost, should surely be prized most highly and be guarded against everything that might endanger its possession and enjoyment. And it is evident from the passage before us, and from other Scriptures, that responsibility is laid upon us to stand firmly in our dearly bought freedom.

What then is that "yoke of bondage" against which such an earnest warning is raised? It is often said that the yoke of bondage is the law; and that idea seems to find support in what Peter said at Jerusalem. We recall his words: "Now therefore why tempt ye God to put a yoke upon the neck of the disciples which neither our fathers nor we were able to bear?" (Acts 15:10). But it should be observed that the great question there was about the *circumcision* of Gentile converts. That ques-tion was raised by certain men which came down from Judea to Antioch and taught the brethren, saying: "Except ye *be circumcised after the manner of Moses,* ye cannot be saved" (Acts 15:1). Moreover, we should observe that the very next verse of Galatians also mentions *circumcision* as being, or as standing for, that "bondage" against which Paul was warning the saints. "Behold I, Paul, say unto you that *if ye be circumcised* Christ shall profit you nothing" (5:2).

The law of the Lord is not a yoke of bondage: for it is "perfect, converting the soul." The commandment of the Lord is not a grievous burden; for it is "pure, enlightening the eyes" (Psa. 19:7, 8). The spiritual Israelite prays: "Make me to go in the path of Thy commandments; for therein do I delight" (Ps. 119:35). And he says moreover: "I will *run* in the way of Thy commandments, when Thou shall enlarge my heart" (id. 32); and again, "I will walk *at liberty;* for I seek Thy precepts"; and again, "I will *delight myself* in Thy commandments, which I have loved" (45, 47). The Lord Jesus promises great reward to those who "*do* and teach" His commandments (Mat. 5:19): and the last blessing of the Bible is pronounced on them "that do His commandments" (Rev. 22:14). Therefore, to keep in the path of God's law is not bondage, but is, on the contrary, to "walk at *liberty*"

Truly then, as it is written, so may we with certainty affirm, that "Great peace have they which *love Thy law;* and nothing shall offend them" (Ps. 119: 165). Indeed, the entire Scripture is a witness to the blessedness of the man whose "delight is in the law of the LORD"; and who in His law doth "meditate day and night" (Ps. 1: 2).

It needs then but slight consideration of the matter to make it clear that the doing of the revealed will of God is not a life of "bondage," but is the most blessed existence imaginable. In the path of His commandments is found all joy, peace, health and fruitfulness; while on the other hand every departure therefrom must cause pain, sorrow and loss. Certainly to walk in the law of the Lord is not bondage; but the reverse. Obedience to God's commands is not bondage. On the contrary, it was disobedience thereto that brought the world into bondage.

The Lord Jesus was the only Man who enjoyed *perfect liberty* in this world; yet every step He took was according to the commandment of His Father. He even laid down His life for the sheep because, as He said: "This commandment have I received of My Father" (John 10: 18). Moreover, He came not to destroy the law and the prophets, but to fulfil (Mat. 5: 17, 18). Indeed, when coming into the world He said: "Lo, I come, in the volume of the book it is written of Me, I delight to do Thy will, O my God; yea, *Thy law is within My heart"* (Ps. 40:7, 8; quoted in Heb. 10:5-7)

Such was the Son of God when here on earth, and He has left us an example that we should follow His steps (1 Pet. 2: 21). We have only to recall then that the purpose of God in leaving us, His children, in this world is that He might conform us to the image of His Son, and the great quality in which, for the glory of God, we should seek to be like God's Son, is *obedience*. For our sakes it is written of Him that: "Though he were a Son, yet learned He *obedience* by the things which He suffered; and being made perfect (through sufferings) He became the Author of eternal salvation to all them that obey Him" (Heb. 5:8, with 2:10). It was through His obedience unto death, the death of the cross, that our redemption was accomplished; and that is the proof that obedience is of supreme importance in the eyes of God. Hence the subtlest attacks of the Enemy have been directed against the commandments of Christ, in the effort to create the impression that the keeping of them is "legality."

The purpose of God to conform the saints to the image of His Son is before us constantly in Galatians in one form of words or another; and this is what we have sought to point out and emphasize. In fact, the main object of the Epistle was to warn against teaching which tended to prevent the *perfecting* of the saints. Paul's intense desire that "Christ be *formed*" in them, tells clearly why this Epistle was written. Can it therefore be supposed that the keeping of the law of God is a thing which would hinder God's work in His people? Nay, but rather *that is the very purpose for which His Spirit is given to them.*

There is indeed a vast difference between those who were "under the law" of Moses and those who are now "under grace." Nevertheless, it would be a serious mistake to suppose that they who are under grace are not subject to the law of God. For it is "the mind of the flesh" that is "not subject to the law of God; neither indeed can be" (Rom. 8:7). The difference between the two classes referred to (those "under law" and those "under grace") is this, namely, that those who came to Mount Sinai had a law given them whereby, in the keeping thereof, they might *obtain life;* whereas we who are come to Mount Zion have been given—not a law whereby we may obtain life, but—*life* whereby we may *keep the law of God.* Briefly, the word at Mount Sinai was "do and live," whereas at Mount Zion the word is "live and do."

But the natural heart of men would ever desire to accept the life and escape the doing. Hence the popularity of that teaching (so pleasing to the flesh) which speaks of the holy law of God, and of the keeping thereof, in terms of disparagement such as to instil into the minds of the saints an aversion towards it. We are deeply convinced that the chief need of the hour is the ministry of faithful men (2 Tim. 2:2), who have prepared their hearts "to seek the law of the Lord and to *do* it, and to *teach in Israel* statutes and JUDGMENTS" (Ezra 7:10). Greatly do the people of God need such admonitions as that of James 1:22, 23; "But be ye DOERS of the word, and not hearers only, *deceiving your own selves.* For if any be a hearer of the word and *not* a doer, he is like unto a man beholding his natural face in a glass; for he beholdeth *himself,* and goeth his way, and straightway forgetteth what manner of man he was." But the Epistle of James, along with other Scriptures vitally important to the children of God, is, according to current teaching, denominated "Jewish," and thus is discredited in the eyes of those who receive such teaching. The fact is that *all* the New Testament Scriptures are for this dispensation, which began with the preaching of John the Baptist (Mark 1:1-3, 15).

Briefly then, the law of God is not the bondage against which we are warned, and is not "bondage" at all. The "yoke" referred to in Acts 15:10, and in Galatians 5:1, is the obligation which false teachers sought to impose upon the disciples in telling them they must perfect themselves in the ways of God through the observance of the now abolished ceremonial features of the Mosaic law. Paul was speaking to children of God when he said: "If *ye* be circumcised, Christ shall profit *you* nothing." The truth the apostle is here maintaining is that Christ is given to us, not only for our forgiveness *as sinners,* but *also* for our being made perfect *as saints.* Hence the force of verse 4: "Christ is *become* of no effect unto you, whosoever of you are justified (*i. e.* are *being* justified) by the law; ye are fallen from grace." This verse makes it quite clear that to be under the yoke of bondage, or to be "fallen from grace," is to turn from God's way of perfecting His saints by the work of the Spirit *in* them, and to seek that end through observance of external rites and ceremonies, which men in the flesh can observe as well as saints of God. With a little attention to this passage of Scripture they who are spiritual will see a great difference between keeping the law of God as His children, in the perfect freedom of *voluntary* obedience, and being *justified by* the law in the bondage of *enforced compliance* with its ceremonial details, all of which are fulfilled in the death of Christ, and hence are abolished. If one who had obtained pardon and life through the grace of God by faith, and had also received "by the hearing of faith" the gift of the Holy Spirit, were to be circumcised he would be forsaking the domain of grace altogether. He would be departing from "the household of faith" and "the law of Christ," for the now abolished features of the law of Moses. He would thus make himself "debtor to do the *whole* law." For, if a man who sought to perfect himself by the keeping of the law should offend in one single point, he would be guilty of all (James 2:10). What this would mean is easily understood. For example, the law required the Israelites to dwell in booths during the feast of Tabernacles. Yet for about a thousand years (from the days of Joshua to those of Nehemiah) had not the children of Israel done so (Neh. 8:14-17). Thus Samuel, and David, and Hezekiah, and Isaiah, and other men of God, broke the law in that one point. Consequently they were "guilty of all," and but for the "everlasting covenant," *which always remained in force* and secured God's grace to all the *spiritual* seed of Abraham, there would have been no salvation for those saints of God. It was, in fact, one of the purposes of the law that all the world *should become "guilty before God"* (Rom. 3:19). Thus the law made it evident that the very best of men is cast upon the *mercy* of God. "For by the law is the knowledge of sin" (Rom. 3:20); so that the "blameless" Pharisee, Saul of Tarsus, had to acknowledge "I had not known sin but by the law" (Rom. 7:7). And, it may be added, neither would we.

⌐ The word rendered "become of no effect" contemplates making void *the work of Christ;* and herein lies the seriousness of the error which Paul is denouncing. Christ is needed for the *entire work of God's grace* in the for given sinner. *No part* of that work is to be accomplished \by the keeping of the law of Moses, or of any other law whatever; for we are "complete in Him," and *only* in Him. We repeat that *our* part, in the accomplishment of God's work *in* us (as well as in receiving the benefit of what He accomplished *for* us) is *faith*—not works. Most certainly we are to obey the law of God as given to us through Christ and His apostles; but *not that we may be perfected in righteousness through our own efforts.* The reasons for our keeping the commandments of God given us by Jesus Christ are, first of all, to show our love for Him (John 14:15); secondly to bring forth fruit unto God (John 15:8); and finally as a testimony to the world (Mat. 5:16). In no sense whatever are we to be perfected as saints of God and children of God by our own works.

Hence, in verse 5, the Spirit is again brought into view in contrast with the works of the law, "For we *through the Spirit* do wait for the hope of righteousness by faith." The meaning of this verse is difficult to fix with absolute precision. That which we look and wait for ultimately is, to be changed into the likeness of Christ at His coming. Thus, in the parallel passage in Romans 8:23, 24, it is said we wait "for the adoption, to wit the redemption of our body. For we are saved in hope," etc But the context of Galatians 5:5 seems to call for a more specific construction, though it may be taken also to embrace the broader and final outlook of the saints. The thought seems to be that in order to be perfected in righteousness we do not *work* under a yoke of religious bondage, but we *wait* through *faith* for that work *to be accomplished in us by the Spirit.* In agreement with this is the apostle's prayer in Ephesians: "That He would grant you according .to the riches of His glory to be strengthened with might *by His Spirit* in the inner man, *that Christ may dwell in your hearts by faith"* (Eph. 3:16, 17).

Those who are under grace have to do, not with the matter of *gaining* a life by their own efforts, but with the very different matter of *living* a life bestowed upon them as the free-gift of God. It is for the proper living, governing, and shaping of that life that "the law of Christ" is given. All life is lived to some definite end or purpose; and the end in this case is two-fold, (1) the maturing, or developing to perfection, of the person who lives the life; and (2) the producing of "fruit." It is the first object that is before us here. The second, that is the producing of fruit in contrast with the works of the flesh, is brought forward in the latter part of the chapter.

Circumcision, even though it was appointed by God Himself, can contribute nothing whatever toward attaining the ends for which eternal life is given to them that believe. Hence the strong statement made in verse 6: "For in Christ Jesus neither circumcision availeth anything nor uncircumcision, but faith which worketh by love." Circumcision is, in itself, absolutely ineffectual. It is of force to accomplish *nothing*. It tends rather to defeat the purposes for which life in Christ is bestowed, because it brings the one who accepts it into bondage to a barren and unfruitful system of vain religious routine. Life is characteristically spontaneous and free; and the freest of all life is life eternal. Hence rites and ceremonies are a positive hindrance. What "avails" (or is *of force*) is *"faith." That* is the indispensable thing. And the words which follow show that faith is not a passive

state of mind, but an active force. It *"worketh."* Again
we are prompted to raise a warning cry against the flesh-
pleasing idea, so wide-spread in our day, that faith consists merely in holding orthodox views concerning the
Person and Work of Christ. One may have the most
correct opinions without having any real *faith.* Believing
God consists, and also shows itself, in *doing what God
says.* The gospel is preached not for passive acquiescence (for the mere assent of the mind is of no avail
whatever), but for *obedience.* (Rom. 1:5; 15:18; 16:
26). Christ is the Author of eternal salvation—not to
all the orthodox, but—"to all them that *obey Him"* (Heb.
5:9). The Holy Ghost is given—not to the orthodox, but
—"to them that *obey Him"* (Acts 5:32). The Lord
Jesus at His coming again will take vengeance—not on
the unorthodox and heretics, but—"on them that know
not God and that *obey not* the Gospel of our Lord Jesus
Christ" (2 Thess. 1:7, 8). If, therefore, faith be not
manifested by obedience to the commandments of Christ,
it is not "faith" at all. And it is a denial of the faith for
a man to engage in the performance of religious observances; for Christ *has not commanded these,* but has on
the contrary forbidden them.

To the same effect are the clear words of 1 Corinthians 7:19: "Circumcision is nothing and uncircumcision
is nothing, but the *keeping of the commandments of
God."* The keeping of the commandments of God is, and
necessarily must be, the great thing in God's eyes. For
the children of God must be *"obedient"* children.
Whence could the contrary idea have come from? In
this same passage (1 Corinthians 7) we have in verse 22

a clear indication of what, according to Paul's teaching, is *liberty,* and what is *bondage*: "For he that is called in the Lord, being a bondslave, is the Lord's *freeman*: likewise also he that is called being free is Christ's *bondslave."*

And once more, in Gal. 6:15, we read: "For in Christ Jesus neither circumcision availeth anything nor uncircumcision, but a *new creature."* As new creatures in Christ we are brought into a new order of things wherein rites and ceremonies and the keeping of days, and other works of law, have no place.

True faith works "by love." Faith is something more than mere zeal or fervor, or activity in a "good cause." It works through *love.* True obedience to Christ is prompted and sustained by love for Him. "If ye love Me, keep My commandments" (John 14:15). "For this is the love of God, if we keep His commandments; and His commandments are not grievous" (1 John 5:3). Activity and zeal *without love for Christ* are of no value in His eyes. And by this we learn the great difference between "the yoke of bondage" and the "yoke" of Christ. His word to those who have come to Him, and who have found pardon and life through Him, is this: "Take MY YOKE upon you * * for MY YOKE is easy" (Mat. 11:29, 30). The taking of His yoke must needs be a *voluntary* act; for He will not force it upon any one. Hence we find ourselves brought again to the vitally important matter of rendering *willing* obedience—obedience "from the heart" —to the law or doctrine of Christ.

The Galatians "did run well," that is to say, they were running well in the way of His commandments at the beginning of their life as children of God. At the first

they were *obeying the truth*. But now they were being
hindered in running the race, and were being turned aside
into a by-path which led to nothing at all. That persuasion which turned them aside did not come from him who
had called them through the Gospel; for he (Paul) had
called them "into the grace of Christ" (1:6). He still
however expresses confidence in them "through the Lord,"
and charges their defection not to themselves, but to those
that were "troubling" them.

Verse 11 indicates the motive of the false teachers who
were thus troubling the Galatians. Circumcision, being
the badge of Judaism, was at that time in favor not only
with Jews, by reason of its close association with their
nation, but with the religiously-minded among the Gentiles as well. Hence to set it aside, to proclaim it of no
avail, was to invite persecution. Whatever be the form
that popular religion may take, it is sure to oppose itself
to "the offense of the cross," and also to manifest itself
in the persecution of those who reject its customs and
ways. The offence of the cross lies in this, that it *separates from the world and all its works,* particularly its
religious works, and works are a prominent feature of all
the religions of the world.

The Lord Jesus Christ said to His brethren (who did
not at that time believe on Him) :—"The world cannot
hate you; but Me it hateth, because I testify of it that
the works thereof are evil" (John 7:5-7). This should
be the testimony also of those who are Christ's. But insofar as we bear that testimony faithfully, we invite persecution from the religious world. Just now the leading
denominations of the world are planning great works of

various sorts for which huge sums of money are being gathered. These works are described as "forward" movements, "world-reconstruction" movements, "new-era" enterprises, and the like. There seems to be no definite plan, but merely a vague and general notion that something great must be done for the reconstruction of the world, and that the results aimed at (whatever they may be) are to be attained *through the agency of the Mammon of unrighteousness* * That the modern man and modern church puts unlimited faith in money, and none at all in the living God (Whose Word is scarce heeded in high and influential quarters) is quite evident. Thus, after having expended vast sums of money in the destruction of the world, it is purposed to invoke the aid of money in the work of rebuilding what men have deliberately set themselves, through the agency of the recent war, to destroy.

But God says that all these works are "evil," and His children may not properly take any part in them. The time is near whereof the four and twenty elders speak, saying:

"We give Thee thanks, O Lord God Almighty, which art, and wast, and art to come; because Thou has taken to Thee Thy great power and hast reigned. And the *nations were angry,* and *Thy wrath is come,* and the time * * that Thou shouldest give reward unto Thy servants the prophets, and unto the saints, and them that fear Thy name, and shouldest *destroy them which destroy the earth*" (Rev. 11: 16-18).

---

*I have lately been informed from a trustworthy source that the great "Inter-Church Movement" now (1920) in progress is being heavily backed by moneyed interests, doubtless as a defence against the Bolshevistic threat concerning "Capitalism." See James 5:1-8.

Meanwhile the world is ready to show hatred and per
secution to those who take the place of separation, because
of the cross of Christ, from all these great things of the
flesh, and who, through the Spirit, do wait for the hope
of righteousness by faith. As to all these vain efforts
of men to perfect themselves, to perfect also a Christless
and Godless civilization and a condemned world, we who
belong to Christ have been set free. In view of current
events the Sixth Chapter of Matthews, especially verses
19-34, is of supreme importance. For our resources are
not in the world, but in God our Father in heaven.
Neither are our prospects in the world; for we look forward to a bright inheritance in the world to come. The
knowledge of a Father in heaven, revealed by His own
Son, has set us free from all dependence on the world.
Our life is not in the world; for it is "hid with Christ
in God." We are here not to engage in the works of the
flesh, but to bring forth the fruit of the Spirit. Let us
stand fast, therefore, in the liberty wherewith Christ has
made us free, and be not entangled again with the yoke
of bondage.

Finally it should be noted that circumcision was "a
token of the covenant" given by God to Abraham, and
was designed to serve as a fore-shadowing of the fulfilment of that covenant through "the Seed to Whom the
promise was made." In other words it was, as distinctly
stated in Colossians 2:11, a *foreshadowing of the cross*.
To the children of God it is said: "Ye are complete in
Him, Which is the Head of all principality and power;
in Whom also *ye are circumcised* with the circumcision
made without hands, in putting off the body of the sins

of the flesh *by the circumcision of Christ"* (Col. 2:10, 11).

Therefore to go back to the rite of circumcision would be to give up the reality for the shadow. Against this error Paul also warns in Philippians 3:2, 3, where he speaks of those who are circumcised as "the concision" (signifying mere mutilation), saying:

> "Beware of the concision. For *we* are the circumcision, who worship God *in the Spirit,* and rejoice in Christ Jesus, and have *no confidence in the flesh."*

XVI

THE WORKS OF THE FLESH AND THE FRUIT OF THE SPIRIT

The practical lessons given in the concluding portions of the several Epistles of Paul to the churches of God are indispensable parts thereof. To them therefore we should give the most earnest heed. For the expositions of truth contained in the first parts of the Epistles were intended to serve merely as a foundation for the practical lessons to the household of faith which the Epistles are written to convey. If therefore our reading and study of Galatians does not result in the carrying out of the commandments of the Lord found in the last two chapters, it will have been all in vain.

The practical lessons of this portion of God's Word are mainly these; *first,* that we should walk in the Spirit, *second,* that we should bring forth the fruit of the Spirit, and *third,* that we should sow to the Spirit.

The liberty into which we are called is that of the Spirit of God. Hence the important warning of verse 13: "For, brethren, ye have been called unto liberty; only use not liberty for an occasion to *the flesh,* but by love serve one another."

This warning is much needed in this day of easy-going tendencies, and especially in view of current teaching which has created in many minds the idea that being "not under the law but under grace" means that, inasmuch as we are assured of final salvation on the merits of Christ's atoning work alone, we are free to please ourselves in this present world. Incalculable harm has been done by this false teaching, which has the effect even of turning the grace of God into lasciviousness, and of bringing the whole doctrine of grace into disrepute. The truth is, and one of the main objects of the present volume is to impress it upon our readers, that our liberty in Christ is very far from being a state of insubjection to the law of God. On the contrary it is a state of *complete subjection* to the law of God, and that in the highest and most spiritual form in which law has been revealed to men. True liberty in Christ is complete subjection to the law of God in that form wherein the Lord Jesus, while on earth, walked continually, which was in His heart, and which found expression in all His words and actions. It is "the law of Christ" in the double sense that it is both the law He has given to the household of faith, and also that by which His own life in this evil world was controlled.

Hence the verse we have just quoted tells us that the "liberty" into which we are called, is in fact a *service,* and indeed the word "serve" in the passage "by love *serve* one another" is the verb-form of the very word, "bondage," used to describe the condition from which Christ has set us free. The exact truth of the matter is that we have been called out of one bondage into another. We are *now* to "serve *one another,"* and *"by love."* This is, in fact, nothing less than a call to live as God Himself lives. We may say with reverence, that God is Himself controlled by the law of love, never acting contrary thereto; for God must needs act in accordance with what He *is;* and God *is* Love.

The next verse enforces the lesson: "For *all* the law is fulfilled in *one word*, Thou shalt love thy neighbor as thyself." This is simple and clear. We cannot misunderstand it.

God requires His children to be like Himself. So we have, in these words, the same doctrine as given by our Lord Himself in Matthew 5:44-58:

> "But I say unto you, Love your enemies, bless them that curse you, do good to them that hate you, and pray for them which despitefully use you and persecute you; that ye may be the *children of your Father which is in Heaven.* For He maketh His sun to rise on the evil and on the good, and sendeth rain on the just and on the unjust. * * Be ye therefore perfect, even as your Father which is in heaven is perfect."

In the Epistle to the Ephesians this supreme law of our Lord Jesus Christ is stated in these words:

> "And be ye kind one to another, tender-hearted, forgiving one another, even as God for Christ's sake hath forgiven you. Be ye therefore followers (literally *imitators*) of God as dear (beloved) children, and *walk in love, as Christ hath also loved us and hath given Himself for us, an offering and a sacrifice to God for a sweet-smelling savour*" (Eph. 4:32, 5:1).

Christ is always the example of what He bids us be and do. In the Gospels we have the record of all He "began both to do and teach" (Acts 1:1). And in this supreme feature of His law, the "service" of love which

He rendered "unto His own that were in the world" was "*to the end*" (John 13:1). He loved us and gave Himself for us. Hence we ought *so* to love and serve one another with all our being. There is no limit to this law of love, for as "He laid down His life for us," so "we ought to lay down our lives for the brethren" (1 John 3:16). And indeed some of God's children have been so completely set free from self and the world, and have been so wholly submissive to the law of Christ, that they have even rendered this full service of love to the brethren.

The words "all the law is fulfilled" (Gal. 5:14) show that while the works of the *law* are set aside, the *law itself* is to be *fulfilled* in us. On the other hand, if we do not fulfil the law of God we shall surely be found fulfilling the lust of the flesh. For we read in verse 16: "This I say then, Walk in the Spirit, and ye shall not fulfil the lust of the flesh."

The works of the law (*i. e.* its rites and ceremonies) offered no protection against the lust of the flesh. These were *not* contrary the one to the other; for we all know by experience that we could quite comfortably go on with both. *But the Spirit coming in makes a complete change.* For the Spirit and the flesh are utterly irreconcilable. Between them is nothing but antagonism. For the flesh lusts (or desires) against the Spirit; but the Spirit also desires against, or in opposition to, the flesh; "and these are contrary the one to the other." Moreover, the Spirit is mightier than the flesh; and by His power fleshly habits and lusts which could not be mastered by our own efforts, or put off by means of works of law, may be overcome. This should be the experience of every child of God; and if the reader is still in bondage to fleshly indulgence or lusts, from which he has not as yet found a way of escape, this Scripture points the way to deliverance, and he may find it through the confession of his own inability to subdue the flesh, the forsaking of his own efforts, and the acceptance by faith alone of God's deliverance through the cross of Christ and the working of the Holy Spirit.

It is evident that in those important verses we have a restatement of the truth presented in Romans 8: 1-4, where we find the same contrast between the flesh and the Spirit, and find also deliverance from the law of sin and death through submission to the law of the Spirit of life in Christ Jesus. In that passage moreover the purpose of God for His children is declared, namely: "That the righteousness of the law *might be fulfilled* in us, who walk not after the flesh but after the Spirit." The fulfilment of His holy law is a matter of the highest importance in God's eyes. Hence, to secure to Himself a people in whom the law might be fulfilled, He sent His own Son in the likeness of sinful flesh, and for a sin-offering, and in Him condemned sin in the flesh; and He then sent forth the Holy Spirit, to dwell in those who believe on His Son, and to fulfil the law in them.

In order that we should not fulfil the lust of the flesh it is necessary that we should walk in (or by) the Spirit. This should be most carefully noted, for it has to do with the *practical outcome* of all God's dealings with us and of all His teaching imparted to us. What then is it to walk *in*, or *by*, or (as in Romans 8: 4 *according to*) the Spirit? Clearly it means in the first place to walk in or according to *the commandments of Christ*. The Spirit is given to us not merely to enable us to *understand* the Word, but to enable us by His power to keep it. Hence walking in or by the Spirit involves the exercise of faith in surrendering our own wills in order that we may be guided by the Spirit; and also in setting ourselves to walk in the commandments of Christ, counting upon the help of the unseen Spirit to enable us to do so.

In promising the Spirit to His disciples the Lord said: "When He, the Spirit of truth, is come, He will *guide* you into all truth" (John 16: 13). We have seen that walking in the truth means *doing* the truth, or in other words doing the Lord's commandments. Hence the ministry of the Holy Spirit includes the giving of that help to the children of God without which we could not walk in the truth. But inasmuch as the Spirit is not seen, it is only *by faith* that we can lay hold of the promised help.

The word "guide," as defining the action of the Spirit, indicates that there is no compulsion exerted upon the children of God, no force *compelling* them to walk in the commandments of Christ. For they are "free indeed," there being nothing but "the love of Christ" to constrain them.

To the same effect are the words of Romans 8: 14· "For as many as are *led* by the Spirit of God, they are the sons of God." This Scripture does not say that as many as are the sons of God are led by the Spirit of God; for manifestly some of them are not walking in the truth, but in their own ways, or in the false ways of the world. But when we find one who *is* walking in the truth, being led by the Spirit of God, that one is beyond question a son of God. Again we see by this Scripture that the Spirit does not *drive* or *compel* the sons of God to walk in the right path; but "guides" or "leads" them, thus leaving room for "the obedience of faith" on their part. There is nothing in the work of the Spirit in us to curtail "our liberty in Christ."

The next verse of Galatians (5:18) is similar to Romans 8:14, quoted above. It reads: "But if ye be led of the Spirit ye are not under the law." They who are led of the Spirit are the sons of God; and the sons of God are not under the law, for they are free in Christ from all that He abolished (legal ordinances included) by His death on the cross.

This verse connects also with Romans 6:14: "For sin shall not have dominion over you; for ye are *not under the law,* but under grace." Sin had dominion over those who were "under the law," for the reason that the law furnished no way of escape from sin's dominion; and for the further reason that the law made apparent the presence of sin in the heart of man, and its overmastering power. Hence the statement that "The strength of sin is the law" (1 Cor. 15:56). But those who are "under grace" have deliverance by faith through Jesus Christ from the dominion of sin, and to them the Holy Spirit is given that *through the Spirit,* but always "by faith," they may do the things that are pleasing in God's eyes, which things are found in the commandments of Christ.

We come now to the well-known comparison between the works of the flesh and the fruit of the Spirit (verses 19-23). The works of *the law* have been mentioned in the preceding part of the Epistle, but this is the first mention of the works of *the flesh* (though its lust is referred to in verse 16). These works (seventeen being specifi-

cally named) are said to be "manifest." And indeed we
have only to turn our eye to the scene through which we
are passing in order to realize that these works of the
flesh are very "manifest" indeed on every hand.

However, it is needful to look somewhat closely at
these words (which a good concordance, as Strong's or
Young's, will enable us to do) ; for it would almost seem
as if the translators had feared to give the real meaning
of some of the Greek words, lest thereby certain things
which are quite common among professed "Christians"
might be condemned. Thus the word rendered "witchcraft" is *pharmakeia,* which does not mean "witchcraft"
at all, but the use of drugs.* This particular one of the
works of the flesh is "manifest" enough, whereas witch
craft is not manifest at all. Very significantly it stands
next in the list after "idolatry"—*i. e.* trusting for deliverance in that which man himself makes.

The words rendered "emulations," "variance," "sedi
tions," are found in 1 Cor. 3:3, being there rendered "en
vying and strife, and divisions," which is a better rendering. Furthermore, the word rendered "heresies"
(which word really means the denial of fundamental
truth) should be "sects." It is, of course, an unpleasant
truth to those who are members of sectarian bodies that
"sects," however venerable and respectable they may be,
are works of the flesh; but such is nevertheless the plain
declaration of the Word of God, and we can but point it
out. "Heresies" are not included in the list of works of
the flesh, but "sects" are included. All the great denominations of Christendom are, in fact, just so many
Ishmaels. That is to say, though they bear a certain

---

*See Pharmakeia, by Dr. D. Treharne. 5c.

relation to the faith, they are not born of the Spirit, but of the flesh, as was Ishmael. And they are true in every way to the Ishmael character.

Of these works of the flesh it is solemnly declared that they which do such things shall not inherit the kingdom of God. This is an application of the statement that "the son of the bondwoman shall not be heir with the son of the free woman." Church-membership does not make a man the child of God, or entitle him to any share in the inheritance. Thus the inheritance is brought to mind again at this point as an encouragement to us to put to death, through the Spirit, "the deeds of the body" (Rom. 8:13), which is simply another term for the works of the flesh. The Kingdom of God here mentioned is obviously the coming Kingdom in glory (Mat. 25:31, etc.). This is distinguished in the Scriptures from the Kingdom of heaven, which is now present, and continues during the time that the King is enthroned in *heaven.*

The Scripture we are studying does not declare that children of God who take part in works of the flesh will necessarily lose the Kingdom; for the words "they who do such things" refer to those who in reality are not the children of God at all. But this Scripture does nevertheless impress strongly upon us the need of dealing unsparingly with the flesh and all its works. Every commandment of our Lord Jesus Christ, beginning with those in Matt. 5:22 and 28, is a sword placed in our hands wherewith we may "through the Spirit mortify (*i. e.* put to death) the doings of the body"; and if we do so, we shall "live" out our days upon earth, bringing forth fruit to the glory of God.

The fruit of the Spirit, is, like Isaac, not a product of

mere nature, even at its best, but comes only *after nature has ceased to act,* in other words after death has put an end to the activities of nature. Fruit is the product of *hidden processes* whereof the secret has never been discovered by man, and which are, of course, far beyond the power of man to imitate. Fruit is, moreover, the *final* outcome, as well as the *chief purpose* of every sort of life which is bestowed by the Giver of life. Hence, before there can be any "fruit," there must be *life imparted,* and the life must be that of the particular kind which yields the desired fruit. And even after the life *is* imparted, it must be developed to its *full maturity.* So we reach in this passage the final object, the great end towards which all God's dealings in grace with His children have aimed from the beginning. And if we have read with any intelligence at all what is written for our instruction in this Epistle (and in other Scriptures also) we will have come to understand that the producing of fruit is far beyond the attainment of the best efforts and strivings of men. Moreover if we know this we shall be prepared to cease from our own efforts, thus making way for God to work in us, "both to *will* and to *do* of *His* good pleasure" (Phil. 2:13).

Fruit is the product of forces which work slowly and quietly; whereas "works" are usually the result of sudden impulses, produced by causes acting upon us from without. The fruit of the Spirit can be produced *only* by the unseen Spirit of God through processes which man is utterly incapable of understanding. Our part, therefore, is to cease from our own works, to abstain from fleshly lusts which war against the soul, and to yield ourselves wholly to God as those who are alive from the

dead, in order that *He* may work in us, through His indwelling Spirit, that which is well pleasing in His sight.
(Heb. 13:21).

"The fruit of the Spirit is love, joy, peace"— Love is
first mentioned in this cluster of nine things which make
up the fruit of the Spirit; and, as we have seen, love has
the first place in the law of Christ. We have also seen
that *divine* love is not a mere sentimental feeling, or an
affectionate longing after a person or thing, but an *active
power,* expressing itself in doing good to others *at its own
cost,* and even to the very sacrifice of life itself. The
first mention in Romans of the Holy Spirit occurs in connection with the first mention of "the love of God."
These are the words: "The love of God is shed abroad
in our hearts by the Holy Ghost who is given unto us"
(Rom. 5:5). This is said of those who, being justified
by *faith,* have peace with God through our Lord Jesus
Christ, and who rejoice *in hope* of the glory of God. Into
their hearts the Holy Spirit comes and sheds abroad the
love of God, which will surely express itself, if we hinder
not the work of the Spirit, in loving service to others.
The character of that love of God which He sheds abroad
in our hearts is described in verse 8 (of Romans 5) : "But
God commendeth His love toward us in that, while we
were yet sinners"—and hence enemies of God—"Christ
died for us."

The practical example of the love of God working out
in the lives of those to whom the Spirit was given is
found in the second chapter of Acts. Peter preached
Christ crucified, risen, and glorified; and he also testified
that He, Christ, "being by the right hand of God exalted,
and having received of the Father the promise of the Holy

Ghost, hath shed forth This, which ye now see and hear"
(v. 33). The words "shed forth" are the same as "shed
abroad" in Rom. 5:5. Then they which heard the message of the gospel were "pricked in their *heart,*" and
they manifested their *obedience* to the gospel by asking
the great question "What shall we do?" In response
thereto they were told to repent and be baptized in the
Name of Jesus Christ for the remission of sins; and the
promise was given that they should receive the gift of
the Holy Ghost. The practical outcome of this, was that
"all that believed were *together,* and had *all things common*"—that is to say, they shared all blessings and benefits, all joys and sorrows, insomuch that they even sold
their possessions and divided them according as any had
need. Thus was manifested *love,* the fruit of the Spirit.

Again in Acts 4:31, 35, after they had all been *filled
with the Holy Ghost,* it is recorded that "the multitude of
them that believed were of one heart and of one soul·
neither said any of them that ought of the things that
be possessed was his own; but they had *all things com
mon.* Neither was there any among them that lacked."

This is the true love of God, which is the fruit of the
Spirit. Hence it is written to the family of God: "My
little children, let us not love in word, neither in tongue,
but in *deed* (*i. e.* acts of love), and in truth." And in this
connection we also read: "But whoso hath this world's
good, and seeth his brother have need, and shutteth up his
bowels of compassion from him, how *dwelleth the love
of God in him?*" (1 John 3:17, 18).

All the apostles give prominence to the great law of
love, which has the supreme place among the commandments of Christ. Peter says; "Seeing ye have purified

your souls in obeying the truth *through the Spirit* unto unfeigned *love of the brethren, see that ye love one another with a pure heart fervently,"* that is to say with entire disinterestedness and with burning affection (1 Pet. 1:22).

James speaks of the corresponding commandment as "the *royal* law," saying: "If ye fulfil the *royal law* according to the Scripture, Thou shalt love thy neighbour as thyself, thou shalt do well" (James 2:8). James also illustrates the meaning of Paul's saying—"faith which worketh by love"—when, in explaining what "faith" is, he says, "Now if a brother or a sister be naked and destitute of daily food, and one of you say unto them, Depart in peace, be ye warmed and filled; notwithstanding ye *give them not* those things which are needful to the body, what doth it profit? Even so *faith,* if it hath not *works,* is dead, being alone" (James 2:15-17). Real faith therefore acts upon the Word of Christ, and manifests itself in the loving service of supplying the need of others.

The apostle John puts strong emphasis upon this commandment, making it the chief subject of his second Epistle, where he speaks of "walking in truth as we have received a commandment from the *Father."* (It is worthy of special note that this commandment is given by the *Father* to the children of His household through the Son.) And he explains this by saying: "And now I beseech thee, lady, not as though I wrote a new commandment unto thee, but that which *we* (the apostles) had from the beginning, that *we love one another"* (2 J. 4, 5). Furthermore the apostle urges us, in this connection, to look to ourselves that we lose not those things which we have wrought, but that we receive a full reward; and he warns that "whosoever transgresseth and abideth not in *the doctrine of Christ,*" whereof the chief thing is to love one another, "hath not God," (verses, 8, 9).

Closely following "love" we find "joy" and "peace," which are produced by the indwelling Spirit. They are mentioned also in Romans 5:1-5, referred to above; and in Romans 15:13, where we have the well-known words· "Now the God of hope fill you with all *joy* and *peace* in believing, that ye may abound in hope *through the power of the Holy Ghost.*"

The passage in which the Lord gives and repeats in various forms His great commandment of love, and in which He urges His disciples to cling to His words, contains also the promise (five times repeated) of the coming of the Holy Ghost (John, Chapters 13, 14, 15, 16). And here we find the promise of "righteousness" (16:8, 10), "peace" (14:27), and "joy" (15:11; 16:20-22). So that we have in this great passage the elements of Paul's description of the Kingdom of God, *i. e.* "Righteousness and peace and joy *in the Holy Ghost.*"

Other fruit of the Spirit mentioned in Galatians 5: 22, 23, are "longsuffering, gentleness, (or kindness), goodness, faith, meekness, temperance (or self-control)." These also are found in the commandments of Christ and are seen to perfection in Him in the days of His flesh; for God gave not the Spirit by measure to Him.

The nine things enumerated in this cluster are sometimes divided into groups of three; but to the writer it seems that to classify them in that way is somewhat arti ficial and does not tend to edification.

"Against such things there is no law." Hence there is perfect liberty in the Kingdom of God for the producing of the fruit of the Spirit. For, as stated in 1 Timothy 1: 9-11, "the law is not made for a righteous man, but for the lawless and disobedient, for the ungodly and for sinners" etc. This refers, of course, to the prohibitory clauses of the law, the many "thou shalt nots," every one of which bears witness to the corruption of the natural heart, and to its tendency to do many things contrary to the mind of God. When one is filled with the Spirit and walking in the Spirit he does not come into collision with any of the prohibitions of the law; he is conscious of no restraints, but enjoys perfect liberty; for "where the Spirit of the Lord is there is liberty" (2 Cor. 3: 17). The law whereby fruit is produced is implanted *in the vine itself;* and the simple conditions of producing the fruit of the Spirit are that we abide in Christ, the True Vine, and that His words abide in us (John 15: 1-17). This means full submission to the commandments of Christ, yet it is as far as possible from a state of legal bondage.

"Against such things there is no law. But* they that are Christ's have crucified the flesh with the affections and lusts." We should carefully observe that it is said—not that they that are Christ's are *required* to crucify the flesh with its affections and lusts, but—that they *have done so.* If so, then the law has been executed (as to them) against the flesh. There is, however, a difference between *crucifying,* and *mortifying.* To mortify is to *put to death* and thus make a full end of. So we are called upon to mortify the deeds of the body (Rom. 8: 13). But to

---

*The first word of Gal. 5:24 is "But," not "And."

crucify is to put in a position where life remains and motion is indeed possible, but much limited and painful. The acceptance of Christ involves, among other things, our putting our old man in the position of one "crucified." In contrast to this we have in the next verse the perfect liberty of the new man who has life and also liberty in Christ. "If we *live* in the Spirit let us *also walk* in the Spirit." One who walks is at liberty; and if we avail ourselves of *this* liberty, then, according to verse 16, we shall "not fulfil the lust of the flesh."

> "Christian, wouldst thou fruitful be?
> Jesus saith: 'Abide in Me.'
> From Him all thy fruit is found.
> May it to God's praise abound."

XVII

FULFILLING THE LAW OF CHRIST

"Bear ye one another's burdens, and so fulfil the law of Christ."

The practical aim of the doctrine of this Epistle (Gal. 6:2) may be seen in the contrasted expressions "not fulfil the lust of the flesh," but "fulfil the law of Christ." The fulfilling of the lust of the flesh is what characterized our former state of bondage to self and sin; whereas the fulfilling of the law of Christ is what properly characterizes those who submit to and *continue in* "the perfect law of *liberty*" (Jam. 1:25).*

It is to be observed that the law of Christ has regard mainly to our relations with fellow-believers. It is a family-law, that is to say, a law governing the conduct of "brethren" to one another. In fact the expression "one another" is of very frequent occurrence in passages that give us the doctrine of Christ. The law of liberty works always for the benefit of others rather than of oneself. For love "seeketh not her own" advantage. On the other hand it will be seen upon brief consideration, that in fulfilling the lust of the flesh men gratify themselves *at the expense of others.* Hence submission to the law of Christ by walking in the Spirit involves a complete *reversal* of the motive of life. In order that there may be a change so complete, we must indeed reckon ourselves to be dead to sin, and alive unto God in Christ Jesus. This is the burden of the sixth chapter of Galatians.

---

*Literally "the perfect law, that of liberty."

Beginning with the last verse of chapter 5 are certain practical directions—commandments of the Lord—which illustrate the subject of faith working by love and the fulfilling in that way of the law of Christ. These verses, which are often slighted, call for our closest attention. It would be good for us indeed to commit them to memory, with prayer that God would bring them to mind and give power to carry them out, when the opportunity presents itself. And we will not have to wait long; for situations occur every day wherein these or like commandments should control our conduct.

"Let us not be desirous of vainglory, provoking one another, envying one another" (Gal. 5:26). Whatever glory a man may attain in this world is "vain" or empty. Yet one of the strongest impulses of the natural heart is to strive after personal distinction. This is the commonest of cravings; and along with it goes the "provoking" of others whom we seek by one means or another to surpass, and also the "envying" of those who surpass us. It is evident that to deny completely, and live in opposition to, the primal impulses and cravings of the human heart, is possible *only* to one who has received the new nature and is walking in the Spirit. This verse alone shows that "the law of Christ" is a heavenly thing, superlatively high above even the law of Moses; although in reality it is but the unfolding of the inner meaning of the words "Thou shalt love thy neighbour as thyself."

There are many passages in other Epistles of like import to the above; such as "Let nothing be done through strife or vainglory; but in lowliness of mind let each esteem other better than themselves. Look not every man on his own things, but every man also on the things of others" (Phil. 2:3, 4). Let it sink into our hearts that these are "commandments of the Lord" which we are to obey; and that although the fulfilment of them is impossible to the natural man (the "flesh"), God is the God of Abraham, the God who quickens the dead, and He has given to the children of God His Holy Spirit for the very purpose of doing in us that which the law could not do (Rom. 8:1-4).

> "Brethren, if a man be overtaken in a fault, ye which are spiritual restore such an one in the spirit of meekness; considering thyself lest thou also be tempted. Bear ye one another's burdens, and so fulfil the law of Christ. For if a man think himself to be something when he is nothing, he deceiveth himself" (Gal. 6:1-3).

It is a most solemn matter to approach a fellow saint in order to deal with him for a fault; and in no task that comes in our way is there more need for grace and spirituality. By this Scripture we are again brought face to face with one of our strongest natural tendencies, namely, the tendency to censure and condemn the brother who is overtaken in a fault. By the law of Christ the "spiritual" saints (none other are fit to deal with such a matter at all) are required to *restore* the erring one (see James 5: 19, 20). This forcibly reminds us that we are in a kingdom in which "grace reigns," and whereof forgiveness without limit is the chief characteristic. It reminds us also that we are so united together in one family and fellowship that the wrong-doing of one is the concern of all;

and that it is in the interest of the entire household of faith to seek the *restoration* of the wrongdoer. An erring brother is to be urged lovingly to seek God's mercy and favor through confession, repentance, and (if the case demand it) restitution. His duty must be brought to his notice "in a spirit of meekness"; and a very significant clause is added, "considering thyself lest thou also be tempted." Let us then keep always in mind that, *whatever the fault may be,* we ourselves are just as liable to commit it as the one who was overtaken therein. It is very easy to forget this. Hence our Lord, in the pattern of prayer He gave, after the words "Forgive us our trespasses as we forgive those who trespass against us," added *"and lead us not into temptation"* (Matt. 6:12, 13). What would we ourselves have done if tempted in the same way? "Wherefore, let him that thinketh he standeth take heed lest he fall" (1 Cor. 10:12).

Where blame, therefore, attaches to a fellow-saint, the law of Christ demands that we associate ourselves with him in bearing the burden thereof. Thus, Daniel, Ezra, and doubtless many another man filled with the Spirit of God and having the mind of Christ, took upon themselves the blame of sins committed by the Lord's people, and confessed them as their own. Thus they followed (though indeed afar off) the example of the Lord Himself, Who bore the burden of all the sins of His people, being even "made sin" for them (though without sin Himself and needing not the admonition "considering thyself"), that *they* might be made "the righteousness of God in Him" (2 Cor. 5:21)

If we could but bear always in mind how dear to the

Lord are each and all of His blood-bought people, and that they are "all righteous" in His eyes because the blood of Christ has cleansed them (Rom. 5:9); and if we could also keep in mind that we ourselves are capable of any fault which a brother may commit; we would indeed in all such cases manifest a spirit of meekness, and show the tenderest consideration for the erring one.

And above all let us give the most earnest heed to the Lord's own words on this subject: "Judge not, that *ye* be not judged. For with what judgment ye judge, ye shall be judged; and with what measure ye mete, it shall be measured to you again. And why beholdest thou the mote that is in thy brother's eye, but considerest not the beam that is in thine own eye? Or how wilt thou say to thy brother, Let me pull out the mote out of thine eye; and behold, a beam is in thine own eye? Thou hypocrite, first cast out the beam out of thine own eye; and then shalt thou see clearly to cast out the mote out of thy brother's eye" (Mat. 7:1-5)

In connection with this subject (that of dealing with the faults of others) our attention is called to the humbling fact that "if a man think himself to be something when he is nothing, he deceiveth himself." One who takes upon himself to censure another assumes thereby a position of superiority. By implication he says: "I would not be guilty of such a thing myself." But inasmuch as each one of us is capable, apart from the grace of God, of com mitting any fault possible to another saint, we are each and all thereby disqualified from passing judgment upon others.

But let each one "prove his own work," that is, let him

test his own doings. "For every man shall bear his own burden." This word (burden) is not the same word as that in verse 2. It might be rendered "load." The thought seems to be that, at the approaching judgment seat of Christ, our "works" will be revealed as to their real character; and in view of that fact we should be giving heed to the defects in our own doings rather than to the defects we may see in the work of others. That such is the sense of the passage is indicatd by 1 Corinthians 3:12-15, where we read that "the fire shall *try* every man's work, of what sort it is." The word "try" is the same as that rendered "prove" in Galatians 6:4.

Verse 6 of our chapter recognizes that there are among the people of God those who teach them in the Word of God; and it admonishes them (the people) to share with their teachers "in all good things." This is an important part of the law of Christ. But we would here call to mind what is often forgotten, namely, that "teachers" are those who instruct God's people *how to behave themselves* according to the Word of God, and not those who merely give them from time to time interesting addresses on Bible subjects.

XVIII

SOWING AND REAPING

Now is the seed time; but soon will come the day of reaping what we shall have sown. Are we redeeming the time? The days may be passing very pleasantly, and we may be even enjoying many tokens of God's favor; and possibly we also are comforting ourselves with the assurance that "the coming of the Lord draweth nigh." But are we seeking grace daily to fulfil the law of Christ, especially in those particulars brought to our attention in this Epistle? It is easy to be misled as to this. One may be spiritually asleep; and the time passes pleasantly enough during sleep. So at this point we have the strong admonition: "Be not deceived (or misled). God is not mocked. For whatsoever a man soweth, that shall he also reap. For he that soweth to his (own) flesh, shall of the flesh reap corruption; but he that soweth to the Spirit shall of the Spirit reap life everlasting."

Once again the sharp contrast between the flesh and the Spirit is brought forcibly to our attention. Each day and hour we are sowing seed. Our actions are of one or the other of these two sorts. In due time the results will all be harvested; and the harvest will *correspond with the seed we sow*. This is as certain as that wheat always springs up from wheat, and darnel from darnel. Nothing is more to be feared by the people of this world than a crop-failure. What a disaster if the farmers should all be deceived for a single season, and should sow the seeds of worthless plants! The error might not be manifested for a long time. But the harvest-time would bring to view the serious consequences when too late to correct the mistake.

Let us then yield our best attention to this solemn Scripture. Let it search and expose all our ways. And if we see, in its clear light, that we have been sowing to our own flesh, let us condemn ourselves *now;* and seek grace, in the little time that remains, to sow to the Spirit by keeping the commandments of Christ. It is by grace alone that we can labour abundantly in God's harvest field; but we may, like Paul, find grace to employ our time and opportunities in such way as to be sure of some returns whereof we shall not be ashamed in the day of reaping. Let us then be "not weary in well doing; for in due season"—the time of harvest—"we shall reap if we faint not." "As we have therefore opportunity let us do good unto all men, especially unto them who are of the household of faith."

The importance of using the seed-time profitably in view of the reaping-time that is fast approaching, is brought before us in other Scriptures. "They that sow in tears shall reap in joy"—for the harvesting season is a time of rejoicing. "He that goeth forth and weepeth, bearing precious seed, shall doubtless come again *with rejoicing,* bringing his sheaves with him" (Psa. 126: 5, 6). This last verse speaks very distinctly of Christ, the "Sower Who went forth to sow," and Who sowed the "precious seed" with sorrow and pain. But He had ever in view "the joy that was set before Him"—the joy of the coming "harvest of the earth."

In Hosea 10: 12 is a stirring exhortation to God's peo-

ple of old when they were in a state of departure from
His ways. "Sow to yourselves in righteousness, reap in
mercy; break up your fallow ground: for it is time to
seek the Lord until He come and rain righteousness upon
you." The righteous acts of the Lord's people, that is to
say, the things they do in obedience to His commands—
doing good unto all men, especially to them who are of
the household of faith—are so many seeds cast into the
ground, over which God watches though they are covered
from the view of men and forgotten; and which, through
the rain of His blessing, will in due time yield a rich
harvest.

To the same effect the apostle James was inspired to
write: "And the fruit of righteousness is sown in peace
of (or *for*) them that make peace" (James 3:18). The
context warns (3:16), as does Galatians 5:15, against
envying and strife, and exhorts us to act as a wise man,
showing his works out of a good manner of life with
meekness of wisdom—the wisdom which is from above,
and which is "first pure, then peaceable, easy to be en-
treated, full of mercy and good fruits, without partiality,
and without hypocrisy." In this passage we have the echo
of the Lord's own words, Who was Himself that "Wisdom Which is from above," when He said:

"Blessed are the meek; for they shall inherit the
earth.

Blessed are they which hunger and thirst after
righteousness; for they shall be filled.

Blessed are the merciful; for they shall obtain
mercy.

Blessed are the pure in heart; for they shall see God.   -

Blessed are the peace-makers; for they shall be called the children of God."

A Final Personal Appeal.

Another personal appeal to the beloved Galatian saints occurs in verse 11: "Ye see in how large letters I have written unto you with mine own hand" (Gr.). Since Paul regarded them as his "little children," would they not pay the greater heed to his message because he took the pains to write it with his own hand, not employing an amanuensis, as was his custom? But this mention of himself brings again to mind those who were seeking to draw them away from him and his teaching. How different their motive from his! They were not seeking the welfare of the saints, nor even the keeping of the law; for though they would compel the Galatian believers to be circumcised they themselves *did not keep the law.* Their object was to make a fair appearance in the flesh by outward conformity to the customs of Judaism, to save themselves from persecution on account of the cross of Christ, and to have something whereof they might boast.

This mention of circumcision prompts another setting forth of the great truth that the cross of Christ is, to every believer in the Lord Jesus Christ, the true circumcision which, not in form or symbol only, but in reality, separates him wholly from the world. We have commented on these verses in connection with the main theme of the

Epistle, and therefore need make here only a brief reference to the context in which they are found. "In Christ Jesus neither circumcision availeth anything, nor uncircumcision, but a new creature." The word rendered "creature" is more properly "creation." The cross of Christ is the end of all that His redeemed people were by nature—in the flesh—for there, in His holy flesh, the judgment (due to ourselves because of what we were by nature) was executed. But "in Christ Jesus" now risen from the dead and glorified in heaven, there is a new life and a new existence, quite free from all the incidents of life in the flesh. This truth is more fully stated in the familiar words of 2 Corinthians 5:14-18, where the death of Christ is imputed to all His people; for "if One died for all, all died." But this was with the object, that "they which live should not henceforth live unto themselves, but unto Him who died for them and rose again." It follows that "if any man be *in Christ* there is a *new creation*. Old things are passed away" (for we are crucified to the old things of the world and the flesh); but "behold, all things are become new; and all things are of God who hath reconciled us to Himself by Jesus Christ."

Here is a mighty truth which is for us to accept by faith, and to live in conformity to it. The death of our Lord Jesus Christ has taken us out of the old creation, saving us in the future from its doom and in the present separating us from its religious customs, rites and ceremonies; and His resurrection has brought us into a new creation, where all things are new, and all things are of God. We can see by the example of Paul and of many others that it is possible by faith to lay hold of this truth, and to conform our manner of life to it. If so, there is for us the benediction pronounced in verse 16: "And as many as *walk according to this rule,* peace be on them, and mercy, and upon the Israel of God."

The Israel of God is no doubt the people which God chose for Himself in Christ Jesus before the foundation of the world, the people who trust in the Lord. "They that trust in the Lord shall be as Mount Zion, which cannot be removed, but abideth forever. As the mountains are round about Jerusalem, so the Lord is round about His people from henceforth, even for ever. As for such as turn aside unto their crooked ways, the Lord shall lead them forth with the workers of iniquity: BUT PEACE SHALL BE UPON ISRAEL" (Ps. 125: 1, 2, 5).

This brings us to the closing words of the Epistle; and very touching words they are: "From henceforth let no man trouble me; for I bear in my body the marks (the *stigmata,* i. e. the *brands*) of the Lord Jesus. Brethren, the grace of our Lord Jesus Christ be with your spirit, Amen."

The troublers were not to trouble him with their insistance upon rites and ceremonies which the Lord had fulfilled and abolished through the cross; for he, Paul, bore upon his body visible scars which he affectionately calls "the brands of the Lord Jesus," that is to say brands of ownership which marked him as the bond-slave of the Lord Jesus.

We take it he was referring to the honorable scars which remained as a witness of the violent usage to which he had been subjected by the persecuting Jews. He says

in 2 Corinthians 11 : 24, 25 : "Of the Jews five times received I forty stripes save one. Thrice was I beaten with
rods, once was I stoned." The law of Israel (Deut. 25 :
3) provided that when the judges condemned a wicked
man to be beaten, there should be given him not to exceed
forty stripes. We see, therefore, that in persecuting Paul
contrary to the law they were scrupulous in regard to the
letter of the law, stopping just short of the limit of forty
stripes.

By some it has been surmised that the marks to which
the apostle referred were duplicates of the nail prints
and of the spear-wound in the hands and feet and side of
the Lord Jesus. But we are aware of nothing whatever
to support such an idea, which apparently is a product of
the superstition of the middle ages, so prolific in imag-
inations of that sort.

It is good to know then, and to be established in the
truth, that we are not come unto the Mount that might
be touched (that is, which it was possible to touch, but
which was death for any to touch, even though it were
but a beast) ; but that we are come unto Mount Zion
(Heb. 12 : 18-22), of which it is written : "For there the
Lord commanded *the Blessing,* even *Life forevermore"*
(Ps. 133 : 3). We have seen that the Blessing, covenanted
long ago to the promised Seed of Abraham, is the Holy
Spirit given to be the "life" of those for whom Christ was
made a "curse."   Psalm 133, from which the above-
quoted words are taken, likens the Holy Spirit to the precious ointment with which the High Priest was anointed,
and which enveloped his entire person in a cloud of frag-

rance.   The significance of this has been already pointed out; but we wish, in closing, to call attention to the practical lesson found in the first verse of the Psalm, in the words: "Behold, how good and how pleasant it is for brethren to dwell together in unity!"—"even together," as the orinigal Hebrew is given in the margin.   "Good" it is for them, and "pleasant" in the eyes of God, that they who are Christ's should live as "one."   For this He prayed (John 17:21); for this He died; for this He lives.   The unity of the Spirit is a precious and a costly thing.   The keeping of it is the fulfilling of the law of Christ.   Let us therefore give all diligence to keep it "in the bond of peace."

Made in the USA
Middletown, DE
14 March 2024

51475952R00117